T0208416

TEACHING YOUR KIDS LIFE'S MOST IMPORTANT LESSONS

ROB HELLER
FOUNDER OF BOOSTKIDS

iUniverse, Inc.
New York   Bloomington

BoostKids
Teaching Your Kids Life's Most Important Lessons

iUniverse books may be ordered through booksellers or by contacting:

iUniverse
1663 Liberty Drive
Bloomington, IN 47403
www.iuniverse.com
1-800-Authors (1-800-288-4677)

Because of the dynamic nature of the Internet, any Web addresses or links contained in this book may have changed since publication and may no longer be valid. The views expressed in this work are solely those of the author and do not necessarily reflect the views of the publisher, and the publisher hereby disclaims any responsibility for them.

ISBN: 978-1-4401-9212-8 (pbk)
ISBN: 978-1-4401-9214-2 (cloth)
ISBN: 978-1-4401-9213-5 (ebook)

Library of Congress Control Number: 2009912702

Printed in the United States of America

iUniverse rev. date: 12/30/09

This book is dedicated to my parents for teaching me the BoostKids lessons at an early age. Special thanks to Charlie Copp, Sherry Johnson, and Jeff Salvino for their work with BoostKids.

Contents

Part I

—

Background and History of BoostKids

The History of BoostKids

I am the proud father of three children: Matthew, 17, Samantha, 15, and Will, 11. Five years ago when Matt was twelve, I went looking for a program that would help develop his self-confidence and character. Now, don't get me wrong; Matt was a well-adjusted kid that did well in school and had friends, but like many children that age, he was shy and quiet. I watched him struggle in group settings with his friends. I also knew that coming into his teenage years, Matt would be experiencing an intense level of peer pressure. I wanted to make sure he was properly prepared to handle the difficult situations that would arise. Specifically, I not only wanted to ensure my son had the ability to understand the risks and normal temptations of teenagers, but the character to resist these and other dangers young people often encounter. More than anything, though, I wanted Matt to be confident and feel comfortable with himself.

Success in life, relationships, and careers typically stems from an individual's people skills and character, not necessarily from academic success. So my wife Wendy and I focused on helping Matt master social graces. Wendy and I knew that little things like handshakes and eye contact would increase Matt's ability to get along with others and earn their respect upon the first introduction. We also knew that instilling a strong moral foundation in Matt would guide his decision-making skills and earn him additional respect among friends, family, and teachers.

As a parent, what would you like most for your kids? Do you want them to excel academically? Do you want them to become star athletes? Those are great attributes, but the one overriding quality most parents say they want for their children is confidence in themselves. The type of confidence I am referring to is not arrogance or snobbery, but comfort with who your child is as a person. Grounded and self-confident girls and boys are more likely to grow into adults that are admired by peers and maintain personal relationships with family and friends.

As I searched for a third-party program to help Matt, I could not find a program that taught the crucial lessons that I knew were important. It was at this moment that the idea for BoostKids popped into my head. I said to myself, "What about creating a formal, yet fun and interactive program that teaches kids life's most important lessons, like meeting and greeting, learning how to listen and ask questions, making eye contact, resisting peer pressure, and respecting others?"

As a businessman and entrepreneur, I have learned firsthand that confidence and character are crucial to establishing and balancing family success, career success, and life success. Yet, during the formative years, there is little formal training for these traits. As a parent, you know confidence and character are important. Yet in today's hectic, fast-paced world, it is hard to teach your kids these people skills, especially when you the parent have so little training and so few resources. As a result, many parents feel somewhat helpless, especially as their children are being negatively influenced by the onslaught of the twenty-four-hour-a-day media and technology culture.

I am the type of person that dreams up a lot of different ideas. And to be quite frank, when I share most of my ideas with friends, family, and colleagues, they are usually met with a courteous, "That's nice,

Rob." In other words, "Your idea is not that interesting, so let's move on to another topic."

However, every time I shared the BoostKids concept with friends, parents, or business associates, they would stop in their tracks, a smile would come over their faces, and they would say, "Now that is a great idea. You should run with it!" Such sincere and genuine feedback was an indication that the idea warranted real action. The energy level I sensed in so many parents was inspirational. In fact, the next time I bumped into these same people, they would say, "Did you ever do anything with that kids' confidence idea you told me about?" Let me tell you, it felt great to respond, "Well, as a matter of fact, yes I have."

Realizing that "concerned parents" like me were everywhere, in the spring of 2003, I mentally committed myself to designing the BoostKids program. I spent months researching character development and social skills. I enlisted the advice, knowledge, and help of teachers, guidance counselors, clergy, successful business people, and child psychologists from around the country. I also turned to everyday parents, including my own, to see what they felt were life's most important lessons.

Today, I am proud to say that many educators, non-profit organizations, child development professionals, and after-school programs use BoostKids. In addition, thousands of parents, grandparents, and guardians have turned to BoostKids to successfully teach their children life's most important lessons. The response has been overwhelming. Kids' lives are being improved every day. I hope you, too, find the BoostKids lessons valuable.

Boost It Up for Life!
Rob Heller

CHAPTER 1

What Picture Do You Have
of Your Children in Their 20s?

As parents, we want to help our kids to achieve success at every stage of life. Just think of the time and money we spend to provide the emotional support and resources necessary to assist our children's goals and endeavors.

I often visualize how I can help my kids to become successful adults. Typically, I try to picture my kids in their mid-twenties. That's the point in life where they will really be on their own (hopefully!) and will most closely begin to resemble a mature man or woman. Now ask yourself, "What do I want my children to be like in their mid-twenties?" I imagine you are a lot like me. You probably want your son or daughter to have some or all of the following traits:

- Close personal relationships with family and friends

- Self-confidence

- Respect of others

- Integrity

The BoostKids lessons are designed to help you instill these qualities and characteristics in your children so they develop and grow into responsible and dependable adults. BoostKids covers twenty-eight lessons. Each lesson teaches a specific manner or behavior that will allow your children to feel more confident around grown-ups and more comfortable with themselves.

Most of the BoostKids lessons are pretty obvious. In fact, I am sure you are already teaching many of them at home. BoostKids is designed to help you instill and reinforce social skills and manners that are vital to your children's development. The program provides you, the parent, with specific teachable techniques, so that one day your children may live the mental picture we talked about earlier. Please don't sit around and simply hope for the best. Realize that you have the power to take control and help your children build the successful lives they deserve.

CHAPTER 2

Launching BoostKids

I made the commitment to develop BoostKids after failing to find a program that could teach my son Matt the life lessons Wendy and I value. To be quite honest, I was not even sure how to get started. After much thought, I decided the best approach was to come up with a list of the lessons that I felt needed to be taught. Heck, I'm a parent, I figured my instincts might be shared by thousands, if not millions, of others out there.

The process began with a pencil and paper. I jotted down lessons that I felt were important. In my first attempt, I came up with probably eighteen to twenty of what would end up being the BoostKids twenty-eight lessons. Most of the lessons were obvious (e.g., teaching kids how to listen and ask questions; teaching kids to say someone's name in the greeting process).

Over the next few months, I added lessons as I began to think of situations and scenarios that would help my children develop into responsible adults. During that period, I was inspired by careful observation of the interactions that took place among friends and relatives. For example, after watching my kids' grandfather, Pop-Pop Albie, joking, teasing, and having fun with not only his grandchildren, but everyone he came in contact with, I realized that I needed to include the lesson "Have Fun."

Another time, I was reminded of watching the movie *Star Wars* with my Uncle Irwin when I was a kid. And that's when it hit me—I had to add "Resist the Dark Side" as a lesson to reinforce "good versus evil" and the importance of resisting temptation. To this day, I have vivid memories of talking with my uncle after the movie. He spoke to me about the consequences of the decisions I make and explained that the good guys win in the long run. By reflecting on lessons I learned from my family members, I realized just how much kids learn from being around loved ones, friends, and other role models.

A major BoostKids theme is the idea that parents must be role models for their kids. Our decisions, temperaments, and actions rub off on our sons and daughters. Kids are like sponges, they quietly absorb personality traits as they observe how people close to them behave. At every turn, parents have to remember that there's a little person watching, with a great, big brain! A brain that is hungry for information, so let's make sure it's good information that we are feeding our kids.

As I developed the program, I also engaged other parents through a series of focus groups to discover what life lessons were important to them. Believe it or not, the issue most often mentioned was teaching kids proper telephone manners. Yes, even today, in the age of cell phones, text messages, and e-mails, parents want their kids to represent themselves and their families with respect when communicating. That just goes to prove that while technologies change, good old-fashioned values rarely do.

Eventually, after much due diligence, the following twenty-eight lessons stood tall in front of me:

- Greeting People

- Eye Contact

- Smile

- Have Fun

- Try New Things

- Don't Announce Your Strengths/Admit Your Weaknesses

- Resist the Dark Side

- Apologize Quickly and Sincerely

- How to Handle Being Teased

First BoostKids Class

In order to refine and test the concept, I began to teach Matt and six of his friends (boys and girls) the BoostKids lessons in a classroom setting. We met once a week for eight weeks. I utilized a number of teaching tools, from direct instruction and lecturing to role-playing skits. In addition, each student was joined by at least one parent. At every stage of the BoostKids program development process, parental observation and feedback was crucial. At the conclusion of eight weeks of classroom instruction, I was astonished at the positive response that was generated. The parents noted remarkable changes in the behavior of their children at home, at school, and in social settings. All the kids had picked up specific techniques that they began to apply in everyday life to make them feel more confident.

After the successful classroom trial, I put the BoostKids program up against the next level of scrutiny. I wanted to prove that the twenty-eight lessons could pass muster with potentially the toughest critics—educators and child professionals. So I began consulting with teachers, guidance counselors, principals, and child psychologists.

In particular, Dr. Harvey Ziff, a child psychologist in Doylestown, Pennsylvania, heard about BoostKids and requested to take a closer look at it. Dr. Ziff, who operates Camp Friendship, summer camp in Doylestown, PA dedicated to developing children's social skills and self-confidence, found the program to be a useful tool for families and children as a starting point for discussion of important life skills, and as a self-directed primer. I want to thank Dr. Ziff and his wife for the recognition and support they have provided BoostKids.

I also want to recognize Charlie Copp, a professional educator. Charlie helped introduce BoostKids to schools and after-school programs. This effort allowed us once again to witness, first hand, the effect BoostKids was having on kids. And once again, the feedback we received was not only amazing, but validating. Parents, teachers, and guidance counselors continue to write us letters documenting the positive influence BoostKids is making in the lives of their children and students.

BoostKids has taken boys and girls that, in many cases, have almost no people skills and very little self-esteem and provided the tools and skills they need to open up to the world.

Let me give you a great example. In a middle school outside of Philadelphia, we conducted an eight-week program with ten kids that could barely look you in the eye or maintain a conversation. By the end of the course, their teachers were amazed at the change. The children gained the confidence to look you in the eye and recite your name throughout the course of a conversation. Parents testified to seeing changes in their kids for the first time in their lives—changes they had sadly come to expect would never occur.

In a Georgia school, BoostKids ran a similar program with similar results. At the onset, the principal directed our attention to a young girl that perpetually walked with her head down and her hair covering her eyes. By the end of the program, this withdrawn young girl had transformed into a confident young woman who walked tall in the hallways with her head held high and her hair pulled back.

The letters, e-mails, and cards from parents of children that we've helped are truly inspiring and unbelievably satisfying. Whether it's watching my son Matt flourish, or reading about somebody else's child thrive, I must admit the feeling is second to none. What motivates me to get up early every day and tell the BoostKids story is the potential to help another parent, another kid, another family.

BoostKids Program

The BoostKids program is a comprehensive program centered on our interactive CD-ROM, which contains a video lesson on each of our twenty-eight people-skill and character-building lessons. There is a companion activity book, a set of practice cards, and audio CDs to provide extra tips and motivation for both parents and children.

Go to www.boostkids.com for more information.

CHAPTER 3

What Makes Kids Confident?

Let's face it, at one time we were all kids. While that's hard for our children to grasp, many of us remember it all too well. Today, as concerned parents, we know how fragile a child's psyche can be growing up. Adolescence was, is, and always will be a difficult stage of life for most kids. The early teenage years, in particular, can prove to be a challenging period.

As our sons and daughters mature, they will experience the gamut of emotions, from social anxiety to newfound feelings for the opposite sex. Of course, most kids find a way to survive puberty's bumpy ride, as they gain confidence through the natural physical and psychological maturation process. But there's plenty of room for improvement. Why not speed up the process of feeling confident by helping your child develop the skills to navigate this difficult time?

The Base: Love and Affection

The foundation of your child's confidence comes from the love and affection that you provide on a daily basis. In fact, it's a very simple formula. If you have ever heard the adage "You get what you give," you know exactly what I'm talking about. The level of emotional development a child ultimately carries throughout life tends to reflect the level of emotional involvement that parents, guardians, and other family members invest in that child. In other words, low doses of love and affection will likely yield low levels of self-confidence and low self-esteem. At the opposite end of the spectrum, high doses of love and affection will likely result in high levels of confidence and high self-esteem.

This is not to say a person is doomed without doting parents. We all know people who have grown up to be perfectly adjusted adults after enduring tough childhoods. I must admit, it is amazing when you see a kid from a broken home become successful in life. But these exceptions do not negate my point concerning the prominent role of love and affection. The odds of a child growing into a happy and successful adult are greatly improved if that individual is raised with devoted caretakers.

They Need Skills!

As children grow, they begin to encounter social situations in which their self-confidence will be tested. At this point, the love and affection they received at home may not be enough to sustain their self-confidence in school and society at large. Love and affection gives kids a great head start, but it might not be enough. To forge ahead and become successful in their interpersonal relationships and careers, kids need additional skills and techniques to aid them in challenging social situations where they lack comfort.

Although a parent's praise and adoration does create a great foundation for building confidence, kids need practical techniques to refine their skills and help them handle basic human interactions. Love and affection may only take them so far. Children need to understand how to effectively deal with others in order to earn respect and become "likable." That's where BoostKids comes in. The BoostKids lessons and techniques can take children that have good foundations through love and affection and launch them to the stars.

CHAPTER 4

BoostKids Philosophy:
People Skills and Strong Character

The fundamental concept behind BoostKids is that true confidence is derived from possessing two primary broad-based qualities:

- People skills

- Character

People skills

People skills are the ability to feel comfortable in social situations and get along with others. Basic human interactions such as chatting with friends, meeting someone for the first time, and conversing with the grocery store clerk require people skills. Effective social skills will afford your son or daughter the opportunity to be viewed favorably by the person or people with whom he or she is communicating.

Strong people skills do not come naturally to everyone, but the good news is that they can be taught. BoostKids covers specific techniques that will allow your children to maximize their people skills.

Character Development

The second area that BoostKids focuses on developing is character. It is very simple why building strong character in your son or daughter at a young age is crucial. Character is one's moral compass of values and beliefs. In order for a child to attain true self-confidence, BoostKids believes that outstanding people skills must be accompanied by the ability to distinguish right from wrong. BoostKids helps parents develop character in children that will allow them to establish a high level of confidence.

Are People Skills More Important Than Character?

BoostKids places equal weight on people skills and character. History is filled with crooks and thieves who had great people skills, but very little character. Some of the best con artists in the world were smooth talkers, but lies and deceit eventually caught up with them. These are not the type of people I want my kids to admire or imitate. And I am guessing that, as a concerned parent, you share my feelings.

On the other hand, we all know people with strong character, who are honest and trustworthy, but lack the appropriate people skills. It's difficult for these individuals to develop relationships because they are unable to connect with others in social settings. If your child is an upstanding citizen, but timid and shy, his or her reputation may suffer. Now, of course, your son or daughter is a good person, but few people will have the opportunity to see that if he or she appears standoffish. In order to be likable, children must be approachable.

Parents that want to help their children to create healthy, long-lasting personal relationships throughout their lives will promote *both* strong people skills and strong character.

Chapter 5

Give Praise—When Deserved!

> WARNING: If you have been conditioned to believe that all children deserve adulation all the time, BoostKids may disrupt your misinformed view of child rearing. Consumption of the words below may cause you to abandon your long-held views of parenting.

The mission of BoostKids is to increase confidence in children by developing their people skills and characters. Specifically, the BoostKids program is designed to help parents teach kids social lessons and techniques that will allow them to develop in these two important areas. BoostKids is *not* designed to tell kids how great they are, especially when they are not deserving of praise.

About twenty-five years ago, a movement to develop self-esteem taught parents to praise their children whether they earned it or not. This began the "feel-good" trend of giving every kid in the league a trophy, instead of just members of the championship team. The BoostKids philosophy is to praise children in order to help build their self-esteem, but only when it is earned.

BoostKids is not about giving kids a false sense of accomplishment. If you try to give your son or daughter the perfect childhood, you will have failed to equip your child for life. Children need to develop the tools to handle the highs and lows that come with each and every day.

The lesson portion of this book covers some very simple, straightforward techniques that will allow your child to develop strong people skills. As opposed to undeserved praise, teaching these specific lessons will allow your child to flourish. Believe me! I've watched Matt's confidence grow leaps and bounds, right in front of my very eyes.

I started working with Matt at the age of twelve, and now he's seventeen and preparing for college. Today, Matt is much more outgoing and comfortable in his own shoes. The poise and confidence Matt has gained over the past five years have propelled him to new levels of performance, scholastically and socially. My son has not turned into a different person—he is simply a polished and refined version of the Matt my wife and I have always known. Let me tell you, as a parent, I am so proud of my son. Thanks to the BoostKids techniques and philosophies, Matt has successfully carved out an identity that is all his own.

CHAPTER 6

Are People Skills and Strong Character More Important Than Being Smart?

One of the reasons I was motivated to develop BoostKids was to dispel the long-held notion that a high IQ and academic success will lead to career achievement and social success. We all know people that are tremendous academic achievers, but lack the necessary people skills to become leaders in their fields or captains of industry. Conversely, we know people that did not do well academically. But because they excelled in the areas of people skills and character, they were able to establish great relationships and career success.

In 1995, renowned author and psychologist Daniel Goleman wrote a revolutionary book titled *Emotional Intelligence: Why It Can Matter More Than IQ*.[1] In a nutshell, Dr. Goleman suggested that emotional intelligence, or EQ, may be more important than the standard measure of human intellect, which is known as IQ. Dr. Goleman defines emotional intelligence as a person's ability to get along with others, empathize, and understand human behavior.

We all know people who are book smart and great test takers but do not have the ability to communicate and get along with people. As a result, emotional intelligence is often more important for generating career success than a person's intellectual intelligence (IQ).

First Job Interview

Think about the typical first job interview. Interviewers tend to focus on the candidate's personality and aptitude for the position at stake, as opposed to grade point average or high school algebra grade. Affable, highly motivated individuals will usually earn the job offer or an invitation to the next round of interviews. In many cases, the name of the college listed on the diploma does not even matter.

Parents have become overwhelmingly fixated on the prestige of the college their children attend. Remember, when all is said and done and it is time to step out into the real world, employers will hire the individuals they feel are compatible with the rest of the workforce. Business decision-makers look for people who will emotionally "fit in" with the culture of the company and be able to relate with its customers.

By developing your child's people skills, you will be providing a head start that will last a lifetime. You will also give your child a leg up in that all-important first job interview.

CHAPTER 7

BoostKids Study

Helping you understand that emotional intelligence (EQ) can be more important than standard intellectual intelligence (IQ) in determining career success is one reason BoostKids is essential to your child's future. Initially, this claim was something I only intuitively believed to be true, so I decided I needed hard data to validate my hypothesis. Eager to support this argument, I decided BoostKids had to engage the business community directly to get real answers. My initial urge was to corral the opinions of corporate CEOs, but I soon backed away from that idea. I realized that if I wanted to mine the most accurate, unadulterated results, I needed to approach the professionals who are in the trenches hiring, firing, and evaluating.

Survey Question

In 2006, BoostKids commissioned a study of over two hundred human resource managers and asked them a simple question:

> *What percentage of someone's career success is attributed to that person's people skills, as opposed to his or her technical knowledge of the job?*

I figured if anyone knew the answer to our question, it was the human resource specialists that witness career launches and careers flops on a daily basis. We were confident that we had targeted the men and women who could provide the behind-the-scenes scoop.

Survey Results

The human resource managers reported that 70 percent of workers' career success can be attributed to their people skills, versus 30 percent resulting from technical knowledge of the job.

The survey confirmed what I had suspected all along. The ability to develop, manage, and maintain professional relationships allows a person to reach full potential and shine. But this holds true beyond the job place. This framework extends into relationships on the home front and throughout life in general. So start teaching your kids these skills now. The earlier you begin, the greater the chances of success.

Chapter 8

Are Parents Focusing on the Wrong Things?

At the expense of people skills and character development, parents have focused a disproportionate amount of their time, effort, and resources toward academics and athletics. I may seem politically incorrect, but academics and athletics have been overemphasized. And the result has been devastating. We are raising a generation of young people focused like a laser beam on themselves. Now, I don't blame the kids; they are simply following the lead of their parents (yes, that means us). I place the blame squarely on the parents. And I am just as guilty as the next parent.

Too many of us get wrapped up in believing our kid is the next Einstein, our kid is the next Michael Jordan, our kid is the next Olympic champion. Truth be told, our kids are special to our families and immediate relatives. But that is all that should really matter. Your children are supposed to be special in your eyes and heart, not in anyone else's. Let's be honest, it's hard to convince your neighbors and your colleagues at the office that your kid is special. Face it, no one really cares, nor should they. It's only important that you recognize your kids to be geniuses and superstars in their own right, because it's your attention that they truly crave.

Yes, we must continue to demand academic excellence and encourage athletic participation, but we must be careful not to become obsessed to the point of delusion. We must strike the proper balance between academic/athletic success and people skills and character development.

Academics

Helping your children accomplish homework tasks and prepare for tests is one of the primary functions of a dedicated and loving parent. Kids need to be able to read, write, and do math to the best of their abilities. More importantly, we all want our kids to be curious, ask questions, and become interested in expanding their knowledge base.

Unfortunately, parents today are spending an exorbitant amount of time and money on academic success. Believe me, I can see how it happens—I do the same with my children. It has become so competitive to get into the "right" college that parents feel pressured into spending however much it takes on tutors and SAT prep courses to ensure that their kids are accepted at one of the "gold-standard" institutions. It just seems to be out of whack. The amount of time that we spend emphasizing test scores and grades to the exclusion of developing people skills and building character is detrimental to our children.

My son Matt is studying now for the SAT. Over the next four months, he will spend ninety minutes a week with a tutor preparing for one standardized test. I wish we could dedicate that much time each week to working on his people skills and developing his character. Unfortunately, the college admission process has become so demanding that parents are forced to worry about their children's letter grades while neglecting people skills and character development.

Under the *No Child Left Behind* federal education directive, schools do not have the time to teach these skills. I have had a number schools interested in the BoostKids program, but they were unable to fit it into their curriculum because their attention is focused on national-level standardized testing.

Athletics

My criticism of academic obsession also applies to the arena of athletics. I am a big believer in competition and physical fitness, but too many parents have gotten caught up in the sports frenzy. I've been athletically inclined my entire life, and even in my late 40s, I still work out five to six days a week. And I'll be the first to promote the benefits sports offer children of all ages: teamwork, determination, and discipline, not to mention a healthy body and a sound mind. But let's face it, most of our kids will not be in the NBA. The chances of our children becoming professional athletes are pretty slim.

Yet, many parents spend endless amounts of energy and money pushing their children in sports. Vast resources are spent on coaches, clinics, camps, and trainers at the exclusion of time and effort developing people skills and character. So my theory is simple. If you can find the time for outside trainers and coaches, you can find the time to work on BoostKids!

Except in some very special situations involving uniquely talented and gifted youngsters, parental priorities are simply out of balance. If you want to know what will have the biggest impact on your child, it's neither academic tutors nor athletic trainers, but the book you are reading right now. The BoostKids principles are guaranteed to prepare your children for life!

CHAPTER 9

Most Important Job, Yet No Formal Training

If you ask parents what their most important "job" is, most will say raising their kids. Yet, unlike in their day jobs, parents have received minimal, if any, training when it comes to child rearing. In fact, we are all basically teaching from gut instinct.

Think about it, for your most important job, being a parent, you have received what amounts to zero education (and no, I will not count the pre-birth Lamaze classes!). Now compare this to the amount of training and instruction parents invest in their day jobs. We are talking about years, if not decades of formal preparation.

Obviously, I am not trying to diminish the importance of a day job. A parent's career is not only necessary to pay the bills, but it also highlights to children the virtues of commitment and sacrifice. But beyond providing financial resources, a dedicated mom or dad serves as the most powerful role model in the life of child. While professional athletes may visually entertain kids, a loving parent stimulates the heart, mind, and soul. Nothing can replace the sound of mother's soothing voice or the touch of a father's reassuring pat on the back.

Just for a second, reflect on the amount of time you have spent preparing for your day job. And for simplicity's sake, let's just take a look at a standard public-school education. Now, if someone merely graduates high school, they have spent considerable time being "trained." The total hours a student spends going from kindergarten through high school add up to roughly something like this:

6 hours/day × 5 days/week × 40 weeks/year × 13 years (K–12) = 15,600 Hours

That's 15,600 total hours of beginner-level training for a day job. This does not even include college, graduate school, or a tailored company-training program. Yet, most parents are winging it when it comes to raising kids, their most important job.

Although most parents do the best they can to teach their kids life's most important lessons, they often do not have the range or breadth of knowledge to teach the techniques and skills necessary to maximize their son's or daughter's potential. I developed BoostKids to help parents like you perform the job that is the most critical—being a parent and raising your children.

BoostKids provides parents the missing pieces of education that were not taught in a classroom. BoostKids showcases the essential areas of social development and provides techniques that parents can use to teach their children life's most important lessons. At the end of the day, great teachers need great tools.

CHAPTER 10

Kids Grow Up So Fast
Now Is the Time to Teach Them!

Robert Orben, the great American author and presidential speechwriter, once said, "Time flies. It's up to you to be the navigator."[2] In my estimation, those brilliant words ring truer now than they ever have before. Think about where you were ten years ago. Do the events of a decade past seem like they occurred last week? Well, for me they do. Recently, Wendy and I were reminiscing about moving into our house when Matt was six months old. Now he is seventeen and a couple of inches taller than I am. It seems as if we just moved into the neighborhood a few years ago. How did Matt get to be seventeen so fast? Where has the time gone?

Just about everyone I know experiences similar feelings about "time flying by." So let's go back to the second half of Orben's statement: "It's up to you to be the navigator." Young kids cannot jump into the "cockpit" if they do not know to operate the controls and read the gauges. Children need help chartering the course of their future. The best way to do so is by safely getting off the ground. And that's the role of a parent—to act as the flight instructor and co-pilot. Now, parents cannot necessarily guarantee a smooth ride, but they can greatly improve their son's or daughter's chances of a successful takeoff.

The proverb "You can't teach an old dog new tricks" is true. It's pointless to try to teach an adult dog how to sit and roll over because it's too late. By the middle to late stages of life, the dog's brain is hardwired.

The same is true with kids. That's why it's absolutely crucial to start teaching the BoostKids principals *now*.

Kids grow up so fast. The older they get, the harder it will be to teach them the BoostKids techniques, traits, and habits. It is much easier to instill the BoostKids lessons today. The sooner you introduce your child to life's most important lessons, the sooner these skills will become second nature.

The mere fact that you are reading this book is great news. You have probably already begun teaching people skills and character one way or another. But now is the time to redouble your efforts with the BoostKids lessons.

CHAPTER 11

Trigger Moment

The BoostKids lessons are not exactly earth-shattering revelations. They were never intended to sweep you off your feet and send a wowing chill up your spine. If I sat here and told you that BoostKids is chock-full of new concepts and keen insight, I would only be kidding myself. Most of the lessons and philosophies behind BoostKids you already know. So my role is simple—to help you reinforce life's most important lessons with your children.

There are certain moments in people's lives when they suddenly realize that action must be immediately taken. This is when an individual finally admits that the idle strategy of procrastination has unraveled. Years of talking about a problem, or worse, simply just hoping for the best, eventually takes a toll. It's at this point that a person decides, "Enough is enough, a new path must be taken." I call these points in time "trigger moments."

Now the last thing you should be doing is wasting time and energy on being angry with yourself because you knew all along what you needed to do, but for some reason, you just never reached the trigger point. Don't beat yourself up. The fact that you are reading this book proves how much you care. Life's fast pace can cause you to lose focus. Sometimes parents get so caught up in the rat race that they fail to take action. A variety of events can vault a person back into reality: a seminar, professional help, or maybe just a friend's advice. I hope that this BoostKids book has created your "trigger moment."

You love your children and I know you want them to be confident and enjoy success throughout their life. Yet, most parents have never really dedicated themselves to teaching the fundamental techniques that will increase their children's people skills and develop their character. Our goal is to reverse that trend and inspire parents to dedicate themselves and their children to the important lessons of BoostKids.

CHAPTER 12

Skills are More Important Than Ever

Today's children face an unprecedented variety of choices, distractions, and temptations. In addition to the sheer number of enticements, there is little doubt that the current generation of young people has been exposed to pressure at an earlier age than any previous generation. And the pressure can be excruciating. So many kids feel that they are being pulled in a thousand directions simultaneously. And worst of all, parents like you and me are often adding, not alleviating, stress. In my opinion, a combination of cultural burdens and vicarious parenting has stunted our children's social skills and character development.

Below are some "disruption factors" that stand between your children and the people skills and character they need to learn.

Technology

To our generation, young people do not seem as social as the boys and girls who grew up in years past. The reason for this change is quite clear: technology. Kids are spending excessive amounts of time in the house staring at a screen. Whether they are surfing the Internet, playing video games, or wasting countless hours watching mindless television, too many kids are drifting off into their own universe. In fact, sometimes they are so engrossed in these activities that they are totally unaware of what is occurring in their immediate surroundings. Have you ever walked in a room, said hello to your son and daughter, and been completely ignored? I know I have!

E-mailing, text messaging, and virtual-reality gaming is overtaking our kids' lives at breakneck speed. And the cumulative effect of these activities is less and less human interaction. I once witnessed my daughter Samantha having a text-message conversation with a friend when they were both in the same room! This lack of face-to-face dialogue and the social dysfunction that follows—i.e., a lack of people skills and character—can be devastating to your child down the road.

In a face-to-face conversation, individuals are forced to think on their feet and react swiftly. Communication tools such as text messages and e-mails (although incredibly efficient and vital to a growing global economy) allow people the luxury of a slow, deliberate response, and oftentimes, no response at all. Even little things, like understanding how the tone of one's voice is interpreted, are critical in your child's developmental years.

Beyond the spoken word, let us not forget the other important form of expression—body language. The advent of many modern communication devices has nearly eliminated our need to worry about displaying the correct body language. Just imagine (and this is not as far-fetched a scenario as you may think) if your children engage in job interviews one day with absolutely no clue about the dos and don'ts of body language. Well, they may be in for a rude awakening, and very few second-round interviews, if they are oblivious to the body-language messages they either conveyed or fail to convey.

A key quality throughout life is self-awareness. Self-awareness is the ability to understand how the world views you. Good examples of behaviors that children should learn to become aware of include voice tone and body language. Unfortunately, most kids do not just naturally figure out these communication skills. It takes an involved, loving parent to teach and instill these lessons so that a child can mature into a confident adult filled with poise and character. You cannot afford simply to hope your child will someday "figure out" the appropriate skills to communicate effectively in face-to-face settings.

Media and Pop Culture

Today's media outlets and entertainment fashion plates put a premium on looking thin and flawless. This puts unneeded pressure and anxiety on young people to look the part and often results in a significant drop in self-confidence when they realize that they cannot fit the "mold."

Pop culture has had a tremendous influence on lowering the standards of proper social behavior. Music videos, movies, and even radio shock jocks encourage young people to be disrespectful and ignore standard protocols of respect and courtesy. I have had it up to my eyeballs with what I call the "ESPNing" of sports. Not to place the blame squarely on the shoulders of ESPN, but on a daily basis, sports-highlight shows deliver into our homes, and sear into the eyes and minds of our kids, pictures of their idols trash-talking and showing up opponents. It has gotten so bad that when a football player makes a routine tackle, he dances, celebrates, and even taunts his opponent.

Like many of you, I have coached my kids' community sports teams. I remember a few years ago, I was coaching my youngest son Will's basketball team. And every time one of the players on the opposing team scored, he would pound his chest and point at the player that was guarding him. And this was only a six- and seven-year-old league!

Heck, I am even fed up with cartoons. I was watching one with my kids recently in which the characters repeatedly insulted each other. All I heard for thirty minutes was, "Hey, stupid," "You're dumb," and "Shut up." Listen, I do not expect television shows to teach my kids the principals of respect; that's my job. But I am now forced to be vigilant in monitoring the disrespect and crudeness in kids' cartoons?

Overly Competitive Environment

Today's world has become so competitive for children. On an absolutely ridiculous scale, unrealistic expectations are being thrust upon our sons and daughters. From an increasingly early age, I hear so many parents bragging that their kid is the best athlete or the smartest student. But here's the really scary part: If I am hearing all this nonsense in public, just imagine the amount of pressure being put on these kids in the privacy of their own homes.

It seems like everywhere you turn, parents are measuring each other by their kids' academic successes, athletic achievements, and college acceptance letters. The need for some parents to live vicariously through their children has not only sent many moms and dads into a competitive frenzy, but also turned our sons and daughters into narcissists. Research shows that today's teenagers and young adults are more egotistical than those who grew up in years past.[3] But can we blame them? If your intelligence, physical appearance, or athletic prowess were constantly being praised and promoted, you too might develop an inflated sense of self. Our children's spending countless hours developing their profiles on Facebook has led to the development of a generation of narcissists.

BoostKids has been designed to help you and your kids combat an unhealthy, over-the-top obsession with good looks, trophies, newspaper clippings, IQ scores, and grade point averages. Instead, we urge you to direct a good bit of attention and focus on people skills and character.

I hope the "disruption factors" reviewed above have created a sense of urgency in you to help your children at an early age overcome the technological, cultural (and yes, even parental) obstacles of growing up in the twenty-first century.

Chapter 13

Are Kids Born with Good People Skills or Can They Be Developed?

People skills and character come more naturally to some children than to others. So, is nature or nurture more important? While there is no doubt that a genetic component plays a vital role in a child's emotional development, humans still have the capacity to learn how to be confident. I can see it with my three kids—they all have different personalities. My oldest, Matt, is shy and quiet, so people skills do not come naturally to him, especially when he meets people in social settings. However, my younger son, Will, can light up a room and connect with everyone.

The BoostKids program is designed to empower children to become comfortable and confident in any environment. Matt has developed skills over the last couple of years that have really boosted his confidence. The comment we get back from friends, relatives, and teachers is, "Wow, Matt has really grown up." This positive feedback energizes Matt (not to mention his proud dad!) and is all due to the life skills he has developed using BoostKids. Matt is living proof that people skills can absolutely be taught and learned, even if they don't come naturally to your child. And we are seeing this time and time again with kids all over the country that have gone through the BoostKids program.

What Creates Confidence?

Gaining confidence can be as simple as setting and accomplishing one small goal. Achieving just one goal can serve as a launching pad. Increasing children's comfort level in situations that require the often-unnerving task of meeting new people or navigating an unfamiliar situation can propel them to conquer bigger challenges.

An analogy would be riding a roller coaster. At first, a child may be scared to even look at a roller coaster, let alone step foot on one. We've all been there—I know I've had the fear myself and so have my kids. But once you get buckled in and finish a few loops around, you think, "Wow! I can do it." After you realize how much fun it is, the fear dissipates and the urge strikes to get back in line and to do it again.

You will find that the BoostKids program generates the same energy and excitement (okay, maybe not exactly the same as a roller coaster, but pretty darn close). Once your children master a lesson or two, they will think to themselves, "Hey, that really works!"

Introducing your children to the BoostKids philosophies and techniques will greatly improve their chances to experience early success in developing people skills. And before you know it, life's most important lessons will quickly become second nature.

CHAPTER 14

You as a Role Model

People always ask me, "What is the best way to teach the BoostKids lessons?" My simple answer is, "We're all kids at heart, so live the BoostKids principles yourself!" Oftentimes, it may appear your kids are not watching you, but they are. You would be surprised how much your children absorb, even though they often seem caught up in their own worlds. They are paying attention, even when you think they are tuned out.

Wendy and I were recently driving in the car with our kids. We started talking about "Tom," a neighbor that frankly neither Wendy nor I like. We ended up speaking negatively about him for quite a few miles. A couple of days later, Matt asked, "How come you don't like Tom?" I immediately realized that I had broken one of the BoostKids lessons—*Don't Talk about Other People behind Their Backs*. As a parent, that is why it so important to live the BoostKids lessons. Children can have ears like sonar when you least expect it.

I learned many of the BoostKids lessons just by watching and emulating my mother and father. So much of the way I approach people and situations is from the life lessons my parents taught me. Years of closely watching their behavior and social tendencies helped me develop good people skills and strong character. That is why it is so important for parents like you and me to live the BoostKids lessons.

When you are in the supermarket, let your kids see you engage in friendly conversation with the checkout person. When your kids see you interacting with strangers or friends, let them see you asking questions, not just talking about yourself. Remember, they're always watching you, so be a role model.

My parents never failed to lead by example. I learned so much from their manners and behavior. If you invest just a little bit of time and energy in being great role model, it will pay huge dividends throughout your children's entire lives. I promise.

Part II

—

The BoostKids Lessons

Welcome to the lesson portion of BoostKids. This section will introduce you to all twenty-eight BoostKids lessons. More importantly, this section will give you guidance and instructions on specific techniques you can use to reinforce these crucial lessons.

Lesson 1:
Greeting People

> **"Strive to be first: first to nod, first to smile,**
>
> **first to compliment, and first to forgive."**
>
> *Author Unknown*

When you meet someone for the first time, your brain subconsciously processes thoughts and renders opinions. You immediately wonder:

1) Would I like this person?

2) Could I be friends with him or her?

3) Would I connect with him or her?

Well, the same questions are being asked about your child. That is why it is so important to help your son or daughter make a great first impression right out of the gate. The human mind computes an impression of someone in mere seconds. There is an old saying "You don't get a second chance to make a first impression," and it is absolutely true. The good news is that there are specific techniques you can teach your children that will help them make a great impression—the first time, every time.

The concept of making a great impression also applies to situations where your child encounters a familiar face or friend. Even if your child is shy or reserved, BoostKids provides simple techniques that will make your son or daughter feel and appear confident.

Suggestions for Effective Greetings

1. Say "Hi" First

When meeting someone, teach your child to be the first one to say hello. Kids tend to be naturally shy, so work with your child to break the uncomfortable pattern of *secretly hoping* the other person will speak first. By saying "Hi" first, your son or daughter will appear confident to adults and children.

Kids find themselves in situations in which they pass by someone they know without saying "Hi." But let's be honest, this is an issue people of all ages struggle with. Many times, kids and adults alike hope the other person has the courage to speak first.

Oftentimes when the other person fails to say "Hi" to us, many of us tend to feel snubbed or offended when, in fact, our inability to say "Hi" likely leaves the other party feeling the same way.

When your child begins to make a sincere effort to say hello first (even if the other person does not reply) he or she will be viewed as friendly, secure, and confident.

2. Always Use People's Names When Saying "Hi"

Simply saying "Hi" is not enough. In order to make the salutation more personal, encourage your child to say, "Hi, John," or "Hi, Jamie." Explain that people value their names and are more easily engaged when they hear them upon the greeting and throughout the conversation.

When individuals fail to hear their names upon being addressed, they will assume that your child has forgotten. If, in fact, your child does not know or cannot remember a name, teach him or her to be honest and politely ask. Once your child has heard the name, he or she should immediately repeat it aloud, "Thanks, great to see you again Chris," and then remember it for the next time.

You know how good it feels when someone says, "Hi," and uses your name. In no time, your children will feel the same way and go out of their way to make others feel special too. It is amazing how these two simple techniques allow anyone to feel and appear confident.

3. Firm Handshake

Teach your child to offer a firm handshake. A weak, flimsy shake that resembles a fish flopping out of water is a sign that your child is not confident. A solid handshake will allow your child to establish instant respect and credibility with adults. Tell your child that you want his or her personality and confidence to be transmitted through a strong (but not crushing) grip. Extending a firm hand says your child is sincere, warm, and pleased to be in the company of others. This is any easy one to develop: just practice until your child gets it right.

4. Stand Tall

Body language speaks volumes about confidence. In fact, studies show body language can account for 70 percent of all communication. Children may be saying one thing with their words, but sending a totally different message with their bodies. People can say, "That's fine," but if they have their arms folded in front of them, you know it's not "fine." Stress how important it is to "stand tall." By keeping their heads up, shoulders back, and bodies upright, your children will signal poise and confidence with their posture. Go ahead and try it yourself right now—pull your shoulders back and hold your head high. Doesn't this simple movement help you instantly feel more invigorated than if you were slouched over?

The bottom line: Standing tall will not only instantly help your child to feel and look more confident, but will communicate to the world, "I'm open to meeting you!"

BoostKids in Real Life:

I have two young neighbors that are about the same age—Jimmy and Eric. As soon as Jimmy sees me, he says, "Hi, Mr. Heller." When Eric sees me, he usually waits for me to say "Hi" first and then just mutters a weak "hey" without saying my name. Now, who seems more confident, Jimmy or Eric? Jimmy does, of course—simply by proactively saying "Hi" first and including my name in the greeting. Just two basic courtesies make a huge difference in how I view each boy's level of confidence.

Tips:

1) Begin practicing the greeting process around family, friends, and neighbors. If you work in a familiar, comfortable environment, your child can achieve success and you can monitor progress.

2) Ask your children not to just say "Hi" to a neighbor, but to include the neighbor's name in the greeting: "Hi, Mr. Smith." Remind them to address neighbors as they would their teachers or school principal, with a Mr., Mrs., or Miss salutation.

3) Ask your children to welcome guests into your home by shaking their hands firmly. Gently remind them that you'll be watching and listening in the background.

Lesson 2:
Eye Contact

> **"Never bend your head. Always hold it high.**
>
> **Look the world straight in the face."**
>
> *Helen Keller*

Many of you have already taught your children the importance of eye contact. So it comes as no surprise that it is extremely important that your children look directly at people with whom they are speaking.

Eye contact conveys respect and interest. If your child looks down at the ground or up in the air during a conversation, the message will be, "I'm bored," "I'm insecure," or "I'm immature." These are the wrong messages.

Eye contact is a sign of confidence. Think about confident individuals you have met throughout your life. Don't they look you in the eye?

As with all the BoostKids lessons, remind your child of your expectations before the skill is necessary in a situation. For example, if you're going to see a family friend, Mr. Wilkes, it is much easier and less stressful to say to your daughter in advance, "Alison, make sure you look Mr. Wilkes in the eye," rather than saying it in Mr. Wilkes's presence. Correcting your child in front of Mr. Wilkes only creates unnecessary tension. Provide feedback in the privacy of your car or home.

The person with whom your child is speaking needs to think that he or she is the most important person in the room. By looking people in the eye, your children will not only exude confidence, but make everyone around them feel like a million bucks. Quite simply, eye contact is a crucial people skill.

Tips:

1) Practice at home. Your child first has to learn to look you in the eye. Challenge your son or daughter to look you directly in the eye for thirty to sixty seconds while talking about two or three things that happened at school. Focusing on this eye-contact drill for just one minute a day will help increase your child's confidence.

2) Don't be afraid to have some fun. On occasion, have staring contests to see who laughs or blinks first. This will get your child in the habit of maintaining eye contact.

Lesson 3:
Smile

> **"No one needs a smile as much as
> a person who fails to give one."**
>
> *Author Unknown*

Teaching your child to smile may not only be one of the easiest BoostKids lessons to teach, it is also one of the biggest difference-makers. Smiling will do two things for your child:

1) It makes your child more appealing to others. Think about having a conversation with a person who looks too serious; that person doesn't come off as friendly. By smiling, your child is communicating openness to people.

2) It helps your child to relax. Wherever you are, however you feel, smile right now. Smiling immediately relaxes you—your shoulders drop and tension eases.

As parents, we have come to understand how much a friendly smile can improve a conversation. So when your child sports a smile, not only will it make other people feel more comfortable, but it will having a calming effect on your child, too.

A smile also happens to be an inexpensive way to improve your child's

appearance. Kids spend so much time worrying about clothes and hair, yet a simple smile will immediately make them more attractive.

The next time your child speaks with a smile, ask him or her to take notice of the other person's reaction. Chances are, the listener will become more relaxed and more interested in your child's thoughts and opinions. In time, your child will be become addicted to showing off those pearly whites.

BoostKids in Real Life:

When my son Matt was younger, he had that "deer-in-the-headlights" look every time he had a conversation with someone. This made the other people realize Matt was uncomfortable and just wanted to get the conversation over with quickly. Because I've continued to stress to Matt the importance of smiling, over time (unfortunately, it took a few years) he has begun to smile much more during conversations. The difference is amazing. Other people feel more comfortable and relaxed around Matt. And, more importantly, Matt feels more comfortable with himself.

Tip:

Practice by standing in front of a mirror with your child. First, engage your son or daughter in a conversation in which you both have non-expressive faces. Then have the same conversation while both of you crack a little smile. Your son or daughter will begin to see how much more relaxed the conversation is with a smile.

Although this exercise may seem silly, your child will begin to understand that the reflection in the mirror is the image the rest of the world sees. Explain that people often interpret moods, attitudes, and personality from facial expressions. Make sure your child sees him- or herself smiling, because that is what everyone else will be noticing.

Lesson 4:
Turn Up the Volume

> **"We always speak well when we manage to be understood."**
>
> *Moliere*

A confident child will speak up and speak clearly enough so other people can hear and understand. The key to effective communication is managing and maintaining voice volume through each sentence. Quite  often, kids start off speaking loudly and clearly, only to have their words trail off.

On the other hand, if your child rushes through the words, what results is a mumble that it is difficult for others to understand. Stress the importance of slowing down and being thoughtful. Mumbling can be a sign of someone who lacks self-confidence or is not confident in the words. Teaching your child to speak with authority and clarity will make that child confident and assertive throughout life.

Tips:

1) When driving with your son or daughter, instead of playing the radio or daydreaming, engage your child in conversation. The sound of the car and surrounding traffic will force your child to speak up so that you can have a meaningful dialogue. Make sure his or her voice does not trail off at the ends of sentences.

2) If you don't already, try to have dinner together more often. This is a great time to get your children to talk and speak clearly.

Lesson 5:
Telephone Manners

> **"Before speaking, consider the interpretation of your words as well as their intent."**
>
> *Andrew Alden*

When we ask parents which BoostKids lesson is the most important, one of the most common answers is telephone manners. Many parents cringe when their kids either answer the phone or make a call. And taking into account the rapid proliferation of cell phones, traditional phone manners are eroding quickly. We are raising a generation of young people that may lack the common etiquette skills necessary to be a successful adult.

The key to establishing telephone manners is pointing out how to have a little bit of friendly conversation. When your child phones a friend, but a mom or dad answers, encourage some friendly general conversation before your child gets to the point of the call. This is a common courtesy that will leave other parents with a positive impression of your son or daughter. Here are some examples:

When Your Child Calls a Friend and The Friend's Parent Answers:

- **WRONG WAY:**   "Is Tommy there?"

- **RIGHT WAY:** "Hi, Mr. Johnson. This is Billy. How are you today? (*Wait for Mr. Johnson's response.*) Is Tommy there?"

When Your Child Answers a Call from an Adult Looking for You:

- **WRONG WAY:** "OK, I'll get him (or her)."

- **RIGHT WAY:** "Hi, Mrs. Furman. I saw your new car in your driveway yesterday. It looks nice. Do you like it?"

Also, remind your son or daughter that it is unacceptable and disrespectful to yell or scream for your attention. Instead, ask your child to quietly find you.

By engaging in polite conversation over the phone, particularly with adults, your child will boost his or her image and confidence. If the adult happens to be your friend, you get the added bonus of having that parent feel like you are raising a conscientious and sophisticated young man or woman.

All parents want their children to be friends with the kid that possesses excellent manners and people skills, hoping that the good behavior and influence will rub off. Who does not want to have kids that learn to act like the most behaved and polite children in the neighborhood?

If they do not realize it, let your children know the impact their telephone manners have made on other parents, your friends, and your coworkers. Such news will immediately boost their confidence and make them feel great.

The subtle skill of making friendly conversation on the phone is a good habit that will boost your children's reputations throughout their life.

BoostKids in Real Life:

I remember a middle-school child named Jessica that was part of a BoostKids class. Jessica was really excited after using the telephone techniques she learned with the mother of one of her friends. The friend's mother made a point of calling Jessica's mom to let her know how mature Jessica sounded on the phone and to invite her to the movies with them. All from just a little friendly conversation with her friend's mother!

Tips:

1) Practice when you are watching television. During commercial breaks, "call" your son or daughter (yes, they will think this exercise is goofy too, but practice makes perfect!) and pretend you are Mrs. Jones, one of your associates at work. Coach your child through the mock conversation and provide feedback on strengths and weaknesses.

2) Keep your ears open. When your child is calling a friend on the phone, provide suggestions on how better to handle small talk with adults and parents who may answer the call.

Lesson 6:
Become a Good Listener

> **"The most basic of all human needs is to understand and be understood. The best way to understand people is to listen to them."**
>
> *Ralph Nichols*

Becoming a good listener may be the most important BoostKids lesson.

The key to effective communication is not speaking, but learning how to listen. Mastering listening techniques is an important skill that will be necessary for your child to succeed in life. Unfortunately, very few people ever master this skill.

Becoming a good listener involves more than learning how to follow rules or instructions. Learning how to listen means teaching your child how to hear what someone is saying. Learning how to listen, and ask questions in the process, is probably the single most important trait in creating a strong dialogue and comfortable atmosphere.

You build more relationships by being interested in others than you do by trying to make others interested in you. Think about that. You build more relationships by being interested in others than you do by trying to make others interested in you. It's so true. People will feel closer to your child, and more comfortable with your child, if you teach your child to show an interest in others instead of talking about his or her own accomplishments and achievements. In today's society, people spend so much time trying to "outspeak," "one-up," and "outdo" each other, that listening has become a lost art.

The ability to be a good listener will help your child in many ways, including:

Developing Relationships

People are more comfortable when they feel the person they are speaking to is listening, rather than trying to talk over them. Think of the people that you like spending time with—don't they listen to what you have to say?

Understanding Situations

When you listen to another person's wants, needs, or desires, you are better equipped to help. If a friend has a problem, you need to listen carefully so you can understand the issue and offer the best suggestion or advice.

Active versus Passive Listeners

In order to master the art of listening, your child must learn to become an active listener. Active listeners focus on understanding what the speaker is trying to communicate. Active listeners do not just allow others to talk; they pay close attention to the words being spoken. Passive listeners do not pay attention to what other people are saying even though they appear to be listening. Passive listeners are not interested in understanding the speaker's message.

Having little regard for a speaker's message is disrespectful and selfish. Teach your child to be a respectful active listener who is capable of absorbing a message and responding in a meaningful way.

Here are some important steps for your child to follow:

1. Ask Questions

A good listener must learn to ask questions. Questions indicate that your child is interested in what others have to say. Asking questions will allow the listener to gather information in order to better understand and potentially help the speaker. Stress the importance of asking *open-ended* questions. These questions are intended to stimulate the conversation, not stymie it with "*conversation-stoppers*" (drab one-word answers, such as "Yes," "No," and "Maybe").

Encourage questions such as:

- "What did that feel like?"

- "What are you going to do?"

- "How will you handle the situation?"

Open-ended questions really get people talking and provide you with more information to better understand the speaker and further the interpersonal dialogue.

BoostKids in Real Life:

Prior to conversations with adults, sit down and develop a series of basic questions for your child to ask. This will best prepare your son or daughter for the real-life situation.

Recently, before going to visit my son's aunt, I sat down with Matt and developed a series of questions he could use in conversation with my sister-in-law. The simple questions were tailored to recent events and details of her life. She wasn't feeling well, so I reminded him to ask her how she was feeling. Her sons were away at college, so I reminded him to ask how his older cousins were doing at school.

When we arrived at his aunt's, Matt asked just those two questions.

1) "How are you feeling?"

2) "How are your sons?"

The next day, his aunt called Wendy, and the feedback she got was amazing. She told Wendy, "I can't believe how much Matt has grown up and how mature he seems." All that praise from just two simple questions! Matt didn't have a long, drawn-out conversation, he simply asked two open-ended questions. When we gave Matt the feedback from his aunt, of course he acted like it was no big deal, but we know he was thrilled. Matt got a sense of the favorable impression that asking questions can leave.

If you get your children in the habit of developing a series of questions, eventually they will initiate the formation of questions to ask on the way to visit a friend or family member. It won't be just you spoon-feeding them the questions to ask.

2. Non-Verbal Communication

"Non-verbal communication" is providing information to someone without using the spoken word. An active listener will keenly observe facial expressions and body language. While words may be saying one thing, a speaker's body language or tone of voice may be saying something completely different. At the same time, it is important that one's non-verbal communication as a listener show that one is engaged and receptive to the speaker.

If your child looks stern or frowns, or walks around with folded arms, the non-verbal message is *So what? Big deal. Who cares?*

3. Do Not Interrupt

Interrupting someone that is speaking shows a lack of respect and total disregard for that person's ideas, thoughts, and opinions. When your child keeps interrupting, the speaker's natural tendency is to stop talking.

4. Make Eye Contact

As I mentioned earlier, make sure your child looks people in the eye during conversations. If your child is looking all over the place, it will deflate and annoy the other individual.

5. Empathize

It is important to understand what another person is feeling, particularly if that person is upset. People appreciate when others take the time to care and show concern. It does not take a lot of effort for your child to show concern. It's as easy as saying:

- "That must have been disappointing."

- "That must have hurt your feelings."

- "You must have been so happy."

BoostKids in Real Life:

As the owner of an employee benefits firm, I always enjoyed taking a new salesperson out on a few sales calls in order to give the person a feel for our company's approach: Listen and ask questions. If we listen and ask questions, the prospect immediately feels more comfortable with our firm's representatives than if we went in touting our services.

Invariably, whenever we recap a new-prospect sales call, the beginning salespeople seem a little startled. They fully expected to hear me tell the prospect about how great our company is. They were always surprised at our laid-back approach of listening to understand what the prospect really wants. But you know what? It has worked time and time again. Our most successful salespeople simply listen and ask question to make the prospect feel more comfortable with us. The salesperson can then be in a much better position to make recommendations about how we can assist the prospect.

The goal of BoostKids is not to turn your child into a super salesperson, but making friends is a little bit like making a sale, not in a bad or dishonest way, but in a way that allows the other person to feel comfortable with you.

Tips:

1) Develop questions your child can ask before a conversation with an adult. Prior to visiting friends or family, come up with one or two straightforward questions. You will be amazed when your child eventually proactively initiates the conservation prep sessions.

2) Remind your children that they were born with two ears, but only one mouth. So they should be listening twice as much as they are talking.

Lesson 7:

How to Handle People That Brag

> **"The most silent people are generally those who think most highly of themselves."**
>
> *William Hazlitt*

For children and adults, it is frustrating to deal with people who brag and boast about themselves. I think we all know from experience that it is extremely difficult to endure conversations with people that are wrapped up in promoting their greatness. We all know these types of people. As soon as you tell a story, they automatically tell a story that tries to top yours.

Although this may be a hard lesson to swallow, teach your child the key to handling people that brag is not to get frustrated, but to have patience. Tell your child that kids who feel the need to "one-up" everyone, and constantly talk about themselves, are usually insecure. Explain that braggers do not feel good about themselves and that their insecurities do not allow them to appreciate the good things other people have achieved.

Once your children realize that bragging comes from insecurity, they will be less likely to brag themselves for fear of coming off as insecure. Plus, more often than not, a bragger's attempt to "look cool" will backfire and end up turning off those they had hoped to impress.

From now on, advise your child to listen when talking with an individual that is bragging. It's not worth getting frustrated. Instead, tell your son or daughter to have patience with braggers and let their actions do the talking. If children feel secure and confident, over time people will discover their strengths and will appreciate the character they display. In fact, there's a good chance that one day down the road, the bragger will admire your child's poise, dignity, and humility.

BoostKids in Real Life:

I remember conducting a role-playing skit in the very first BoostKids class we ever held. I secretly instructed one kid to brag to another kid. Then I sat and waited for the chain reaction to unfold. The first one said, "I scored five goals in yesterday's hockey game." We then asked the other kid what the proper response should be. I wanted to see the reaction of the other kid so I could demonstrate the proper way to handle people that brag. Of course, the other kid came back saying, "Well, I scored six goals."

That's the way most kids handle people that brag. They try to top each other's stories.

Tip:

Ask your child about specific kids that brag. Ask what they brag about. Help your child realize that bragging stems from insecurity. Teach him or her to avoid the temptation of trying to top someone else's story.

Lesson 8:

Say "Thank You"

> **"Silent gratitude isn't much use to anyone."**
>
> *G.B. Stern*

Most of you have raised your children to say thank you. I'm sure you do it all the time: "Now say thank you to Mrs. Jones."

But while most parents instruct their children to say thank you, many don't teach the proper way to say thank you. The proper way is with sincerity and enthusiasm. So, don't just say:

"Thanks."

Instead, extend a warm:

"Thank you so much, Mom!"

There is a big difference between muttering a dull "thanks" and saying "Thank you very much!" with a lot of pep and feeling behind it. If you teach your son or daughter to be truly grateful, other people will know your child is genuinely appreciative. Remind your child that a sincere thank you also increases the chances that the other person will do something nice again in the future!

Ultimately, little gestures such as expressing gratitude with enthusiasm will make a big difference in how your child is perceived.

Tips:

1) Take note of the "thank you" offered by your children. Make sure they are not just saying, "Thanks," but expressing gratitude with sincerity and enthusiasm. Correct an unenthusiastic "thanks" right away, and made sure your child provides a heartfelt "Thank you very much."

2) Thank each of your children at least once a day so that they can see and hear how it is done.

3) Each week, ask your kids about situations in which they said, "Thank you." (For example, "Thanks for holding the door.")

Lesson 9:
The Glass Is Half-Full, Not Half-Empty

> **"Whether you think you can or think you can't, you're right."**
>
> *Henry Ford*

Few among us enjoy listening to negative people. There is an old expression that goes, "Look at a glass as half-full, not half-empty." This saying helps remind us to have a positive approach to life. The person that sees the glass as half-full typically has a happy demeanor and positive outlook on the future.

We want our children to see the good in people and situations. When they look at a half-full glass of lemonade, we want them to think, *Wow, look at all that lemonade*, not *Who drank half of my lemonade?* We do not want to raise our children to be pessimists that see the glass as half-empty.

Teach your kids to "think positive" and look at the glass as being half-full in every situation. Children who are full of optimism are confident because they are focused on accomplishments, not failures.

Build confidence in your children by teaching them to appreciate and cherish their family, friends, and health. The more positive and confident your children become, the more friendships they will develop and the more success they will achieve.

BoostKids in Real Life:

Living life by the "glass-is-half-full" philosophy can inspire you and those around you. Here's a great example.

One time at the end of a tough day, I was talking with a young woman named Monica in my office. I was in a bad mood and feeling sorry for myself because our firm had just lost a major account; my frustration showed. A few minutes later, I received an e-mail from Monica and was blown away. Every once in a while, I pull it out to give me inspiration. It reads:

> **Try to have a good night, Rob. If you can't make today a slam-dunk day, just think of it as a chance for a rebound. Regardless, we will get the 2 points one way or another!**

I asked Monica the next day about the e-mail. I told her how inspirational it was and asked her how she developed this mentality. Her response:

> **"My parents raised me to realize today may not be good, but if you believe and think positive, things will always work out."**

Hopefully, Monica's e-mail also motivates you. As a parent, realize that you have the unique ability to develop your child's positive outlook.

Tips:

1) Ask your child to think of a recent "negative" event. Then explain how to view it as positive.

   A good example might be the letdown your son or daughter suffered when he failed to receive the exact new pair of sneakers he expected, or she didn't get the bicycle she wanted. Explain that they should be grateful for the gifts they received. Ask them if they realize how lucky they are, compared to so many children with nothing.

2) Share a story of a similar event that happened to you when you were a child.

Lesson 10:
Give Compliments

> **"One kind word can warm three winter months"**
>
> *Japanese Proverb*

Compliments make everybody feel great. Think about how good it feels when a kind word is tossed your way. Compliments not only make the recipient feel good, but they enable a new level of comfort and trust to be built in a relationship. Unfortunately, most kids struggle with compliments because they are in the stage of life when they feel bragging is a better route to acceptance.

Teach your child that spreading kind words builds relationships and friendships. It is one thing to tell your children that they need to give more compliments because it is the right thing to do, but when you explain compliments will help them make friends and keep friends, it becomes a whole lot easier and more effective. Who doesn't want to be liked by more people?

Complimenting others displays your self-assuredness. Typically, insecure people have difficultly praising others. Below are some everyday situations where your child could provide a compliment:

- "Nice play!" when a teammate performs well.

- "Your shoes are awesome," if a friend or sibling gets a new pair of sneakers.

- "I heard you got an A on the test, great job!" when a friend or sibling does well in school.

It's one thing to give a compliment. But it's another to really mean it. So, please make sure your child gives compliments with sincerity. Compliments, without conviction in your voice, sound disingenuous. Encourage specificity when compliments are given. For example, your child should say, "I really like that shirt" instead of, "You look nice."

Compliments can also be non-verbal. Think of a "high-five" or a "pound fist." These non-verbal actions can make kids feel just as good as if they were verbally praised by their peers.

Get your children to step out of their comfort zones and give compliments. Remind them that the best way to impress people is to show you are impressed by them.

Tips:

1) Ask your children whom they have recently complimented. Point out that each compliment not only made the other person feel good, but also probably strengthened the relationship.

2) Ask your child to compliment three people in the next twenty-four hours and report back.

3) Give your child at least one compliment a day (if deserved— remember what you just read about faking it!)

4) If you hear your child offer a compliment, take him or her out for a treat. But there is one caveat—the compliment cannot be for you. Hearing "Dad, you look great today" has cost me way too many unnecessary ice creams. Try to force your children out of their comfort zones by telling them they have to compliment a non-family member.

Lesson 11:
Accomplishing Goals

> **"If you doubt you can accomplish something,
> then you can't accomplish it."**
>
> *Rosalynn Carter*

The mind is an amazing tool. If used properly, it can help a child accomplish almost anything. If your children mentally picture themselves accomplishing their goals, eventually these pictures become part of them. If a child keeps one of these pictures in mind, over time that picture becomes reality. The key is to nourish your children's minds with positive thoughts, positive reinforcement, and a disciplined routine.

How to Accomplish Goals with Kids

1) *Sit down with your child and think of a goal that child can achieve within the next thirty days. The goal could be getting an A on a test, becoming a better musician, or trying to be more patient with a younger brother or sister.*

2) *Write the goal down. By writing it down, your child will begin the process of reinforcing the goal. Place the goal somewhere your son or daughter can see it each day. Put it in as many places as*

they would like—the more the better! Tape it to the mirror, put it on your child's school notebook, or place it on a desk at home. Put the goal where your son or daughter will be reminded every day.

3) *Immediately do something with your child to accomplish this goal. Now your child has officially committed to the goal. For example, if getting an "A" on a math test is the goal, start studying, or pick a time when your child will be 100 percent committed to studying.*

4) *Children need to keep goals fresh in their minds throughout the day. As soon as they wake up, they should think of the goals. When they go to sleep, they should think of the goals.*

5) *Do not let any negative thoughts interfere with your children's belief that they can accomplish their goals. Remind them to picture themselves accomplishing the goals.*

6) *Failure is not an option. Help your children do what's necessary to accomplish their goals. This means they must practice, study, and put full effort into their goals.*

7) *Your children will accomplish their goals if you help them stay committed to their plans and if you are committed to them.*

8) *As you and your child reflect on an accomplished goal, do not just focus on the achievement itself, but on the skill set and discipline that was learned. This blueprint for success will lead your children to tackle bigger and bolder goals.*

Positive thinking triggers confidence and confidence triggers the drive, energy, and determination to accomplish goals. Successful people never let negative thoughts flood their brains and disrupt their focus. Permitting negative thoughts to enter the mind creates a self-fulfilling prophecy—one subconsciously not only expects failure, but awaits failure.

If your children believe in themselves, they can accomplish any goal. Make sure positive thoughts about specific goals are the first ones they think about when waking up and the last ones they think about before going to sleep.

Tips:

1) Set a goal together that can be accomplished over a relatively short period of time (one month or less).

2) On a daily basis, review what your child did that day to get one step closer to achieving a goal.

3) Routinely monitor, measure, and encourage progress. Think of yourself as the referee and the cheerleader.

Lesson 12:
Treat People with Respect

**"We must learn to live together as brothers
or perish together as fools."**

Martin Luther King, Jr.

Teaching children to respect others has become extremely difficult in today's day and age. Our sons and daughters are being raised in a society in which it has become acceptable to be disrespectful.

Many individuals that work with today's youth (educators, social workers, coaches) all say the same thing: deteriorating societal values have taken a toll on children.

So what's a parent to do? The key is to constantly work with your children and show them how important it is to be respectful of others. Let them know that you will not tolerate anything less.

At some point, we have all been treated poorly or been made fun of. We know how hurtful, and even humiliating, this can feel. When children make fun of someone by exploiting that person's weaknesses and vulnerabilities, they are purposely trying to tear the person down to make themselves feel superior. Such behavior is unacceptable and must be eliminated.

Kids will often make fun of others when they are in a group setting. They assume that putting someone else down will make them look "cool." Many times, when a child tries to embarrass someone else, the child is the one who looks foolish.

Remind your children that we all have weaknesses. And if they choose to be mean and disrespectful, they will end up being treated the same way. On the other hand, if your children treat people with kindness and respect, they, too, will be treated with kindness and respect. Remember, we get what we give. When your children make an effort to build up someone else's confidence, they'll be building their own simultaneously.

BoostKids in Real Life:

I'm a mentor to a fourteen-year-old boy, Chris, through the Big Brother program. The Big Brother and Big Sister programs are terrific. So many kids out there need guidance. I do it to not only help a child in need, but also to show my own kids the importance of giving back and helping others.

Chris used to tease classmates as a way of dealing with his own insecurities. He struggled to show respect, particularly to his teachers, but as I have consistently talked to him, Chris has begun to improve. I often remind Chris that he hates it when other people don't show him respect, so he should stop treating people the same way. Chris has really improved his social skills and is like a member of our family now.

Tips:

1) Ask your kids to name a person or two that they were kind to at school or around the neighborhood. Then ask them to think of a time that did not treat someone with respect. Discuss how it must have made each person feel.

2) Share stories with your children about people that you have treated with respect and those who have done the same for you.

Lesson 13:
Don't Talk about Others behind Their Backs

> **"There is good in everybody. Boost. Don't knock."**
>
> *Warren G. Harding*

Way too often, kids talk about friends and classmates behind their backs. And sadly, this issue extends beyond kids. Many adults also find themselves indulging in gossip at work or around the neighborhood.

Kids tear down their peers in order to feel better about themselves. This approach often backfires (a familiar theme). There are severe ramifications to speaking negatively about others. Typically, the offenders end up bruising their own images more than that of the people they target.

People who are upbeat, positive, and willing to praise others are viewed as secure and confident. People have a greater respect for those who build up others than they do for those who trash and tear down.

If someone is talking to your child about another person behind that person's back, advise your child to avoid joining the discussion. At this point, your son or daughter has a few options: Change the subject, ignore the speaker, or let the speaker know that talking about others could end up damaging his or her own reputation.

BoostKids in Real Life:

We all know that gossiping online creates a record that can be passed around, leaving a digital footprint that can severely stain your reputation in the process. Unfortunately, that happened with my daughter, Samantha. She said something negative about someone online and it not only got back to the other girl, but that girl's mother. That wasn't a fun call for my wife, Wendy, to receive from the other girl's mother. Samantha learned a tough lesson the hard way.

Don't let your children make the same mistake. Remind them that online conversations are permanent records and can cause permanent damage to your image.

Tips:

1) Do not set a bad example by talking negatively about other adults, neighbors, and relatives in front of your children.

2) Ask your kids about rumors being spread at school and how they handle someone gossiping about a classmate.

Lesson 14:

Do Something Nice! It's Addictive!

> **"Kindness in words creates confidence. Kindness in thinking creates profoundness. Kindness in giving creates love."**
>
> *Lao Tzu*

When your child does something nice for someone, it does two things:

1) First, and foremost, it makes other the person feel good.

2) And second, it makes your child feel good about him or herself.

Simple, nice deeds will not only strengthen your children's reputations and relationships, but will make them feel invigorated as well. Doing something nice for a friend, relative, or classmate will help your child as well as the other person. Kindness puts people in great moods and makes them want to repeat the cycle of generosity over and over.

Sometimes a small gesture requires a small sacrifice. But the pleasure and happiness generated by that gesture often overshadow whatever you gave up.

For example, let's say a boy and his younger brother notice there is one cookie left on the tray. Instead of reaching for it, the older boy offers the cookie to his younger brother. In this case, the good feeling the big brother experiences by allowing his little brother to eat the cookie is much greater than the taste he would have enjoyed for couple of seconds.

Small gestures create a domino effect. Once you do something nice for someone, that good feeling you get by doing something nice becomes addictive, making you want to do something nice for someone else.

BoostKids in Real Life:

In the BoostKids classroom training courses, before the end of every session, we ask the children to do something nice for someone else before the next class. We then talk about the experiences at the start of the next class. It doesn't take kids very long to realize that kindness is a win-win.

Tips:

1) Request that your son or daughter perform two nice deeds each day and then discuss them with you at the end of the day. The acts of kindness can range from helping a friend, to complimenting a teacher, to having a conversation with a classmate who is shy and does not have many friends.

2) Talk to your kids about the people you have been nice to (at work, out in public, etc.). In addition, talk about being the recipient of random acts of kindness.

Lesson 15:

Have Patience

> **"You are educated when you have the ability to listen to almost anything without losing your temper or self-confidence."**
>
> *Robert Frost*

One trait that is hard to teach in today's society is patience. Most children want instant gratification. What they want, they want now! While it's a great virtue to be ambitious, kids must have patience if they hope to fulfill their goals and desires.

Children need to strike a balanced approach between taking action and expecting immediate results. Patience is about dedication, persistence, and self-control. All the lessons we have covered in BoostKids require these traits—whether your child is listening, handling a bragger, or respecting others. As a parent, you need to help your child temper frustration and harness the power of patience.

Although I must admit that out of all the BoostKids lessons, having patience is the one that I struggle with the most.

BoostKids in Real Life:

I recently took Matt and Will to a Philadelphia Sixers basketball game. We were driving to the game in a lot of traffic and I became quite frustrated, aggressively beeping the car horn and changing lanes. I wasn't handling the situation with poise and dignity, to say the least. That's when Will, my eleven-year-old, said from the back seat, "Dad, BoostKids! BoostKids! You have to have patience." He was right. Getting aggravated accomplished absolutely nothing. As it turns out, we got to the game in plenty of time.

An Example of Having Patience

One time to work with your child about having patience is when you promise something and just don't have time to get it right away. Suppose you promise your son a new bike. Most likely, he is going to be chomping at the bit to get his hands on it. We have all been that age and understand the jubilation. But the problem is not the eagerness; it is the demands and expectations of having the bike *now*.

Many times, a lack of patience will get the best of a child, leaving him or her unable to "back off." When the hassling becomes relentless, it turns the whole process into a bad experience. At this point, negotiations are pointless and you must unleash your unilateral parental powers. Demand patience and warn of the consequences that will unfold if the complaining does not stop. At the same time, explain to your son that if he calms down, his patience will be rewarded with a brand new bike. But remind him that it is his decision. He can behave and end up with a new bike or complain and learn to live with the old bike.

Tip:

Point out times when your child was not patient; let her or him see that getting upset really didn't help the situation.

Lesson 16:

Be Honest

> **"Speak only the truth. Act with only the best intention. Once you get into the habit you can really live by this code."**
>
> *Author Unknown*

Dishonesty is a good way to lose friends and ruin relationships. Most people have the ability to realize when a child is lying. Body language almost always reveals deceit. Some people refuse to make eye contact, or glance away, while others begin to stutter or become fidgety with their hands and feet.

And recovering from a lie can be extremely difficult. Regaining an individual's trust can take years, if it is not lost entirely.

When children lie, most of the time it backfires and ends up making them look and feel foolish. Dishonesty can cause serious damage to a kid's reputation.

Do Not Lie to Cover up a Mistake

It is very common for children to lie about something they did to avoid punishment. We all know what happens next. You find out they lied and end up much angrier, and the punishment becomes more severe. Encourage your children to admit they were wrong and apologize when they make mistakes. Most people are very forgiving and more than willing to accept an apology. The hurt that they feel due to a mistake is far less than the hurt they will feel if they find out your child tried to cover it up with a lie. Many times, people see through a lie and become much angrier than if they had been told the truth from the beginning.

BoostKids in Real Life:

Once, Will broke a lamp in the house. He initially said he didn't do it, but we later found out that he did. Apparently, a soccer game had broken out in the living room when Wendy and I weren't around. Of course, his punishment was much more severe than if he had just told us the truth when we first questioned him.

Think about something your child has done wrong. Maybe your child hit a sibling, spilled something on the floor, or failed to tell the truth. Of course, you wouldn't have been as upset if your son or daughter simply admitted the wrongdoing right away. Children need to know that lies and cover-ups disappoint you more than the mistake that was originally made.

Honesty is the glue of all strong relationships. That is why it is so important to work with your child early in life about the importance of telling the truth.

As with all BoostKids lessons, you need to be a role model. If you lie or bend the truth to your friends, what is that teaching your child? Remember, our children are always watching us.

Tip:

Review examples with your child about times he or she lied to cover up a mistake. Point out how much angrier the dishonestly made you than the mistake itself.

Lesson 17:
Don't Let Little Things
Bring You Down

> **"Don't let life discourage you; everyone who got where he is had to begin where he was."**
>
> *Richard L. Evans*

It is challenging, but we cannot allow life's day-to-day hassles to defeat us or our children. Facing strict deadlines and demands on our time, many of us overreact to the curveballs that life throws. Not only is this behavior unacceptable, it is a poor example to set for our children. It is important to remember that these little hassles rarely have a significant effect on our lives. Most obstacles are easily overcome and long forgotten by the end of the day, let alone weeks or years down the road.

Kids have to learn to accept that although each day brings new challenges, they have the power to overcome them. And the more confident and secure your children become, the more equipped they will be to conquer the challenges that life presents.

Think about successful people you know. Most of the time, they tend to possess the mental and emotional strength to shrug off frustration. When a problem arises, work with your child to take it in stride, assess the situation, and figure out a solution.

Tip:

Ask your kids to share with you three times they were frustrated or upset in the past few weeks. Point out that those issues are probably long forgotten by now. Explain that self-induced anxiety only creates more pressure.

Lesson 18:

Feel Good about Yourself

> **"I was looking outside myself for strength and confidence, but it comes from within. It is there all the time."**
>
> *Anna Freud*

Throughout history, the teenage years have proved to be a very difficult period as the human body is changing and maturing. Today's society puts a huge premium on physical appearance and material wealth. As a result, young men and women put an unhealthy amount of pressure on themselves. Such pressure can lead to anxiety, depression, and a host of mental and physical disorders.

Children need to learn to temper their expectations. Although it is easier said than done, we have to teach our kids that beauty lies within. Your child's self-confidence is not determined by clothes, bodyweight, or looks, but by caring actions and a positive attitude. A sound heart, mind, and soul can never be stolen or replaced.

I'm sure you are asking yourself, *How can I prevent pictures of beauty and opulence from driving my children crazy?* As parents, we might not be able to stop the obsession, but we can certainly reduce the madness by stressing and living the following values:

Like Yourself First

Kids, especially teenagers, place too much stock in the idea that if they look good they will be happy. It is much more important to feel good about yourself on the inside than about how you look on the outside. While that will be hard for them to believe right now, they will understand one day.

To feel good, you need to be a confident and caring person. If kids do not respect themselves, they will never find happiness and peace. Teach your kids that if they treat people with love and respect, the whole world will view them as beautiful, handsome, and successful.

Do Not Get Caught Up with Today's Media Creations

Very few people look like fashion models and movie stars. Educate your children that celebrities are far from perfect and their imperfections are often masked by technologies such as airbrushing and screen stretching.

It is also important to teach your children that their self-worth is not based upon material possessions or media expectations. Explain that what the media portrays as "in" today will be "out" within a few weeks or months. Encourage them to build their confidence through kindness and compassion.

Become Healthier and More Energetic

Although you do not want your kids to become obsessed with how they look, there are certain steps your child can take in order to look and feel better. Here are some ideas for helping your son or daughter achieve a healthier and more rewarding life:

1. Exercise

Our children are doing a lot of sitting around these days. And what are we doing about it? Very little! Too many of us are allowing our kids' health to deteriorate.

Years ago, kids were outside running and playing. Today, kids are inside playing video games and eating junk food. To counter this sedentary lifestyle, we must motivate our kids to get off their duffs and participate in physical activities. The benefits of exercise are undeniable: kids become healthier, stronger, more energetic, and even mentally sharper.

It is extremely important that your children begin exercising and getting in shape now. They need to develop healthy habits that last a lifetime. To keep your children physically active, you can:

- Limit their computer and television time.

- Encourage participation in community sports (or just walking a few laps around the neighborhood).

- Set a good example: exercise with light weights, stretch, and do floor exercises like push-ups or sit-ups. Ask them to join.

BoostKids in Real-Life:

Will just started a program on his own initiative: He waits for me to get home and then runs on the treadmill and lifts light weights with me a few days a week. By doing this at eleven, he is developing a pattern that will follow him the rest of his life.

You need to set the stage. If your children do not see you physically active, it becomes much harder for them to establish good exercise habits. I urge all of you, if you are not physically active, get started as a family. Child obesity has reached epidemic proportions. Extra pounds on a kid can lead to a variety of ailments, now and throughout his or her adult life.

---

2. Hygiene

A confident child is well groomed. This may sound obvious, maybe even ridiculous, but bathing daily, brushing after meals, and clipping one's nails are important habits that will allow your child to make a good impression.

3. Nutrition

It is important to introduce healthy foods to your children when they are young. When kids learn to enjoy fruits, vegetables, and low-salt foods early in life, they are much more likely to carry those dietary habits into adulthood. In addition, a good, nutritious diet leads to increased levels of energy and increased performance academically and athletically.

> **BoostKids in Real Life:**
>
> *Although my mother taught me many of the great BoostKids lessons, she also allowed me eat an unlimited amount of junk food. I have a sweet tooth today for candy, cakes, and anything sugary that has been really hard to break. I hate to make it sound as if I am throwing my mother under the bus, but had she stressed healthier eating as a kid, I might not be addicted to sweets.*

Encourage your child to develop healthy living patterns of diet and exercise that will last a lifetime.

4. Rest

It is also very important for your child to get a good night's sleep. Eight hours a night will help your son or daughter feel refreshed in the morning and well prepared for school. Rest is crucial aspect of a child feeling and looking their best.

5. Appearance

Fair or not, people will judge your child upon the first introduction. On one hand, you want to allow your children to be their own people and develop their own style, but you need to balance this with reality. Certain looks are completely out of bounds. You must teach your children that there is a right way to dress and a wrong way to dress. All the complaining and tantrums in the world will not change that fact. While you may be very lenient in what you allow your children to wear around the house or out with friends, you need to enforce an appropriate dress code when it comes to school, religious services, or family functions.

Teaching your children how to dress is much more serious than it sounds. If you fail to be tough, one day they may end up embarrassing themselves in a job interview.

Tips:

1) Ask your kids what they like and dislike about themselves. If they dislike a physical attribute that cannot be changed, explain to them that is what nature intended. If it is something that can be changed, like weight, help them develop sensible diet and exercise plans.

2) Tell your kids what you disliked about yourself as a kid. Explain how you dealt with the problem and grew up to be happy and successful. Sometimes, kids just need a little bit of reassurance.

3) Be a role model when it comes to eating healthy, getting plenty of exercise, and dressing well. The more you do it, the more likely it is that your kids will do it.

Lesson 19:
Don't Be a Complainer

> **"You can overcome anything if you don't bellyache."**
>
> *Bernard M. Baruch*

Most people don't want to be friends with people that are constantly complaining. No one will want to be friends or hang out with a child who is constantly complaining. Most people don't want to hear about these minor problems. Why? Because people have their own problems! Now, of course, we are not talking about sharing a major problem with you, a teacher, or a close relative. Children  must be taught to seek the counsel of a parent or trusted adult when a serious problem or issue arises. What we are talking about is the moaning and groaning over small issues that everyone has to deal with.

If you have children who are addicted to drama and looking for sympathy, let them know that they are neither special nor cursed. Explain that day-to-day problems pop up in everyone's life. Work on developing their emotional and mental toughness. Explain that being tired, having a headache, performing poorly on a test, or facing hours of homework are minor problems. Let your son or daughter know that everybody has burdens to deal with, so no one is particularly interested in hearing about theirs.

Think about adults you know who complain non-stop. It is tough to be around them because they want to bring you, and the rest of the world, down in the dumps with them. People want to be lifted up, not brought down by constant complaining.

Tips:

1) Sit down and review with your child any recent complaining episodes. Suggest that the complaining really didn't solve anything. Point out that most of the time, people really aren't interested in other people's minor problems.

2) Set a good example. Do not allow your children to hear you complain about the little stuff.

Lesson 20:
Create Your Own Identity

> **"The man who trims himself to suit everybody will soon whittle himself away."**
>
> *Charles Schwab*

In order to fit in, many children mimic their friends and copy the habits of the kids they deem to be "cool."

While it may be true that imitation is the greatest form of flattery, it often fails to win the respect of others. Contrary to the belief of most young people, respect is earned by those with the courage to establish their own unique identities, not those who simply follow a crowd.

So talk to your children and explore their interests and passions. Ask them about the hobbies and courses of study they enjoy. In addition, introduce them to pursuits that they may not be familiar with, such as music or reading.

If your daughter plays basketball, make sure her participation is genuine, that she is not just playing because all her friends are.

Instill in your children the courage and confidence to venture down the path that appeals to their senses and plays to their talents and strengths. Over time, they will begin to realize that the "cool kids" are the ones that blaze their own trails.

> **Tip:**
> Encourage your kids to take up their own pursuits, not just because everyone else is doing something.

Lesson 21:

Improve Your Mood

> **"The greatest discovery of my generation is that man can alter his life simply by altering his attitude of mind."**
>
> *James Truslow Adams*

At the drop of a hat, kids can easily get down on themselves or feel emotionally deflated. A host of causes include: a disagreement with a parent, a fight with friend, a poor grade on a test, or failing to receive an invitation to a party. Such events and incidents can leave a child sad, mad, or both.

Children need to realize that they have the ability to control their moods and emotions. Unfortunately, too many young people allow the emotion of the situation to control them. By learning a few techniques, your children can take ownership of their moods.

According to Martin Seligman, Ph.D., a professor of psychology at the University of Pennsylvania, the emotion of feeling down is not triggered by a situation per se, but rather by an individual's "inner voice."[4] The "inner voice" dictates how our bodies and emotions react to information that is being processed by our brains. For example, if someone is mean to your child, it is not the act of cruelty that makes your son or daughter upset, but the "inner voice" telling them they should be upset.

Positive thoughts and self-confidence will enable your children to temper their "inner voices," allowing for a more stable emotional and physical response to almost any situation, whether it is degrading, embarrassing, or upsetting. So teach your children to learn to channel the *positive* side of their "inner voices."

The *negative* side of the "inner voice" can send your child destructive messages, such as:

- "This problem is only going to get worse and it might last forever."

- "This problem is all my fault."

If you work with your children to help them tap into the *positive* side of their "inner voices," they will become equipped to approach difficult times more confidently:

- "I have the ability to overcome this problem."

- "This problem will not last forever."

- "This problem will not affect other aspects of my life."

When your children begin to comprehend and embrace the power of the *positive* side of their inner voices, they will begin to manage the tough situations in their lives better. Successful people learn how to allow the *positive* "inner voice" to dominate their thought processes.

Once your children learn to control their "inner voices," they will be better prepared to tackle life's biggest obstacles.

BoostKids Teaching Example:

Michael and Zach fail to receive an invitation to Julie's party. Both feel upset and left out of the loop because most of their friends have been invited. However, there is a striking difference between how each boy handles the disappointment.

Michael becomes extremely upset and distant. He manages to convince himself that no one likes him and he will never have good friends. Unable to keep his mind off the party, Michael becomes upset and spends the rest of the day isolated in his room. Michael has become fully consumed by his negative "inner voice."

Zach, on the other hand, calls on his positive "inner voice." He is able to reduce the sting of the party snub when he realizes that he is not the only person left off Julie's invitation list. Zach also recalls the good time he had Sarah's party a few weeks back. By the end of the day, Zach starts playing ball with his younger brother in an attempt to move onward and upward.

Tips:

1) Ask your kids about a recent situation or confrontation that made them upset. Explain how they can quickly win back control of their mood by controlling their "inner voices."

2) Ask your kids about the other kids at school. Find one who is calm, cool, and collected, and one who breaks down rather easily. Ask them about the characteristics and qualities of each child. Explain that confidence may be the difference between the two classmates.

Lesson 22:
Be Passionate

> **"Fill your life with as many moments and experiences of joy and passion as you humanly can."**
>
> *Marcia Wieder*

We all naturally gravitate toward people that are passionate and full of energy. So why not help increase your child's "magnetic pull" by teaching him or her how to inject more passion and energy into daily life. It's not as hard as it might sound.

What does your son or daughter enjoy? Is it sports, music, reading, or amusement parks? When children describe the things they love to do, they tend to perk up a few notches. Kids become more physically animated and verbally expressive when describing fulfilling activities. Teach them that this enthusiasm needs to be carried over to other aspects of their lives.

Everyone is born with a personality, but each personality contains different levels of passion and energy. So, if your son or daughter has a low level, don't feel the pressure to turn the dial all the way to high, that's not the goal. The goal is to notch it up one level at a time.

For example, think of your child on a scale of 1 to 5 with "1" being someone without much passion and energy and "5" being someone with a tremendous amount of passion and energy. If your son or daughter is a "1," the goal is to turn your child into a "2," if he or she is a "3," try to get to a "4." You get the idea—a steady, gradual approach makes the growing process manageable and attainable.

You need to promote the activities that fuel your kids' passions. Think about it—your children are consumed by mandatory obligations. But their passions are totally voluntary. It is their introduction to liberation and independence.

Encouraging your children to pursue their passions will not only help them build their self-confidence, but will also help them become more engaging individuals. The more interest you show in your children's pursuits and passions, the more enthusiastic they will become when speaking and listening to others.

Teach your child to use words that convey liveliness and excitement when dealing with people, such as:

- "Awesome!"

- "Fantastic!"

- "Incredible!"

These convey more passion and excitement than boring words and phrases: "okay," "fine," "not bad," and "pretty good."

People feed off those who are excited to be living life. Most people can sense passion and energy immediately. When your child walks into a room, there should be a special bounce in his or her step that suggests confidence.

Tips:

1) Talk to your children about their likes and dislikes. Let them see how their passion and energy levels increase when they are talking about their favorite subjects, sports, hobbies, and classes. Teach them to infuse more of these feelings in everyday conversations.

2) Stand in front of the mirror with your child and have him or her say, "Yes," then say, "Yes" again, but this time with more passion and energy. Then one more time, again raising the energy level. Your son or daughter will probably make fun of the exercise and turn it into a joke, but will get the idea and begin to feel the energy.

3) A common technique with actors is to envision an imaginary line between them and their audience, where it's their job to bring the crowd across the line to really feel the emotion that is being projected. Have your child tell a story and try to get you to cross the imaginary line. Once kids incorporate the routine of visualizing this line, it gets them thinking how they can create passion and energy in their daily lives to connect with friends and family.

4) Set a good example. Be excited about life. Introduce your children to your hobbies and passions. Do not pressure them to follow in your footsteps.

Lesson 23:

Have Fun

> **"When you have confidence, you have a lot of fun.
> And when you have fun, you do amazing things."**
>
> *Joe Namath*

It is very easy for a busy parent to forget about having fun in everyday life. Raising a family, going to work, and paying the bills requires intense focus and a no-nonsense attitude. But while parental responsibilities are nothing to take lightly, we can go overboard. Some of us have become so uptight in day-to-day life that the anxiety and tension is rubbing off on our children.

We tend to get so wound up about minor issues that we never take the time to realize how much stress we're transferring to our children. As a result, not only are your children not learning how to relax and have fun, but they can begin to feel your tension.

Think about it—as an adult, you probably enjoy the company of people who know how to have fun. I would venture to guess that you go out of your way to avoid spending time with people who are uptight and full of complaints. Well, our kids do not deserve any less. They need parents with upbeat attitudes and the ability to let loose now and again.

Please, learn how to sprinkle some more fun into your life. Not only will it positively influence your children and improve your familial relationship at home, but it will also help your children's future relationships. All in all, your children will be better prepared for life when they understand how to strike a balance between having fun and being serious.

BoostKids in Real Life:

In our family, Pop-Pop Albie leads the way in terms of letting loose and having fun. Whether he is at a birthday party, a holiday celebration, or a summer cookout, Pop-Pop Albie is always in a terrific mood and ready for a good time. The man simply knows how to enjoy life and make the people around him feel special. I have never met someone who has generated more laughs and put smiles on more faces. Being in Pop-Pop Albie's presence always reminds me of the need to have fun in everything you do.

Tips:

1) Remember to smile more, joke more, and do more fun activities with your child.

2) If your daughter is an athlete and has been struggling to perform well recently, remind her to stay loose and not be so hard on herself. Let her know that the pros often break out of slumps by remembering how to have fun.

Lesson 24:
Try New Things

> **"The way to develop self-confidence is to do the thing you fear."**
>
> *Williams Jennings Bryan*

Life is all about new experiences, but many children pigeonhole themselves by believing they only like certain foods, sports, or school subjects. They fail to realize that life offers many other great flavors, activities, and  academic pursuits. As a parent, it is your responsibility to open up your child's mind, body, and palate to new discoveries.

The challenge is helping kids break out of their all-too-confining "comfort zones." Create an environment in which new opportunities are bountiful. The only way to truly know if your children like or dislike something is to encourage (and sometimes coerce) them to try it.

All children should:

- Try riding a roller coaster. Nothing gives a kid more confidence than overcoming a fear.

- Try international foods that they have only "heard" were bad.

- Try different sports. You never know when and where athletic talent will be discovered.

BoostKids in Real Life:

There's nothing that builds memories like a family vacation, so we all went to Jamaica. What struck me was how incredibly friendly everyone was. Everywhere you went, the response was, "No problem, mon," or, "I'll take care of it, mon." Not just the people at the resort, but across the whole island. Everywhere I went, I noticed the most upbeat people I have ever seen. I was practically blown away by Gary, the hotel doorman. He knew everyone—from the hotel guests to each and every hotel employee. Gary always had a smile on his face that made everyone who crossed his path feel great. It really made me wonder, what makes so many people on this island was so friendly and carefree? Maybe there was something in their approach I could learn. My first thought was (and I'm sure you're thinking the same thing): It's a beautiful island, with great weather, of course there's less day-to-day stress.

So I decided to ask around and find out the answer. I started out by talking with Gary. His answer blew me away and profoundly changed my approach to life. Gary said, "No mon—it's not just because we are on this beautiful island that everyone is friendly." He proceeded to tell me he has problems just like the rest of us: His daughter has a rare disease that may be life threatening; he is concerned about his job because a new management company just took over the hotel; his car just broke down and he's not sure he has enough money to get it fixed. "No, mon, I have the same problems everyone else has; just because it is beautiful here doesn't make everyone friendly."

"The reason I am like this," *he proceeded to tell me,* ***"is because my mother is like this, my father is like this, my uncle is like this. I was raised this way, as were most people on the island. It's the only way we know."***

That's when it hit me: I needed to become more passionate, have more fun, and try new things. Only this way would I set a proper example for my own kids. Despite how stressful and hectic life was, from that moment on, I was determined to set an example by enjoying and living life to its fullest.

Your kids absolutely need to see that you are excited to live life. If they see you constantly down in the dumps and cranky, how do you expect them to become passionate, full of energy, and enjoy life?

That conversation with Gary literally changed my life. This lesson not only applies to your child, but to your enjoyment of other activities as well. I now go to more concerts, exercise more (I took up additional sports like tennis), and see my friends more often than I did in the past.

Your children are watching you. Show them the way.

Tips:

1) If you go out for Italian every Friday, surprise the family next time by going out for Thai or Indian food.

2) If your daughter is an avid athlete, sign her up for music lessons. If your son is a classical pianist, sign him up for Little League baseball. If they hate it, do not worry! It's all about expanding their horizons and allowing them to draw their own conclusions.

Lesson 25:
Don't Announce Your Strengths— Admit Your Weaknesses

> **"You can determine how confident people are by listening to what they don't say about themselves."**
>
> *Brian G. Jett*

We all haves areas in which we excel. We also have areas in which we struggle. In order to feel secure and confident, it is important that your children understand where they are naturally gifted and where they have to work harder to improve.

Don't Announce Your Strengths

Your children's gifts, talents, and strengths speak for themselves. If people do not praise their ability, there is no reason for your children to go out of their way to promote themselves. People respect those who do not boast about their skills.

Admit Your Weaknesses

Conversely, if your children need to improve in a subject or a sport, they should learn to admit it to for two reasons. First, admitting a weakness is a springboard to dedicating oneself to improvement. And second, honesty and humility will earn the respect of friends and peers.

Two Avenues:
Admitting the Deficiency or Becoming a Defeatist

While it is important that your children admit their weaknesses, they must be careful how the message is delivered. There is a fine line between candor and self-pity. If your children open up about their weaknesses with a defeatist attitude, they will begin to believe that they can never improve upon them.

Example:

If a child is not very good at baseball, the difference between admitting weakness and embracing defeat might go like this:

> **Defeatist:** "I'm not very good at baseball. I will always be worst player on the team."

> **Optimist:** "I'm not playing well, but I'm going to practice to get better."

The optimist not only acknowledges the need for improvement, but fully expects to become a better baseball player as a result. The defeatist reeks of self-loathing and negativity.

BoostKids in Real Life:

My son Will is a decent athlete, but he is not as good at basketball as he would like to be. For a long time Will refused to admit that his skill level was below average. Instead, he tricked himself into believing he was better than his performance suggested. After almost every basketball game, he would inflate his statistics. If he had four points, he would tell himself, and others, that he scored eight points.

I spent a lot of time working with Will on admitting to himself, and his friends, that he needed to improve his basketball skills. After Will finally came to grips with his limitations on the court, he decided to practice longer and harder. Now, instead of wasting time pretending to be what he's not, Will is channeling his energy on improving his shooting, dribbling, and passing.

Helping Will to admit his weakness was like taking a giant weight off his back.

Tips:

1) Ask your kids about their weaknesses and their plans to improve. If they struggle to admit any weaknesses, work with them in reverse. Ask them where they excel. You can then figure that their lowest-rated strengths are indeed the weaknesses they did not want to admit.

2) Share stories with your kids about the weaknesses you have overcome and the weaknesses you currently face. Inspire them with your openness and honesty.

Lesson 26:
Resist the "Dark Side"

> **"Tis one thing to be tempted, another thing to fall."**
>
> *William Shakespeare*

"Good versus Evil" is the central theme of the *Star Wars* movies. And as many of you know, the bad guys were dubbed the "Dark Side." These films portray the temptations of abandoning a principled and humble life for one filled with corruption and power.

In real life, situations occur every day in which your child is seduced by the proverbial "Dark Side." We are not talking about anything on the scale of taking over the universe, but rather the hard choices that kids encounter each and every day. Likely scenarios (here on Earth, that is) include:

- Your child fears being stamped with the "not-cool" label by refusing participation in an illegal or immoral act.

- Your child faces a difficult test and has an opportunity to cheat.

- Your child considers blaming an innocent student to avoid punishment.

Submitting to temptation may give children a temporary good feeling, but will leave them unhappy and regretful in the long run. In addition, such decisions will negatively affect their reputations in school and across the community. Simply lecturing your child that a behavior or decision is *wrong* does not always hit home.

For example, your child needs to understand that getting an A instead of a C is not worth a tarnished personal image or a false sense of academic success. Explain that *earning* a C is more honorable than *cheating* for an A.

This lesson is much easier said than done, but repeat it to your child as many times as you have to: "The key to true happiness is choosing right over wrong." Lying, cheating, stealing, and vandalism will never earn your child respect, only integrity will.

Tip:

Rehash a time or event where your kids got into trouble. Remind them that although the transgression may initially have felt good, the eventual punishment and feelings of guilt were not worth a few moments of pleasure.

Lesson 27:

Apologize Quickly and Sincerely

> **"An apology is the superglue of life. It can repair just about everything."**
>
> *Lynn Johnston*

Nearly every child has said or done something to hurt, upset, or offend a friend, classmate, or family member. And the best way for a child to fix the situation is with a timely and sincere apology. This is similar to the thank-you lesson. While many parents have taught their kids to say, "thank you," few have taught them to say thank you with authenticity. The same philosophy applies to apologies. Most parents have taught their children to utter the obligatory "I'm sorry," but they have not stressed the importance of issuing the apology quickly and with sincerity.

Think about times you have gotten mad at your child. I am sure that, on more than one occasion, you have let your anger flow. And then, when you failed to hear a quick apology or a sincere one, you just erupted. When a child learns to offer a genuine apology immediately, it cuts off the second wave of anger. And as a result, life around the house can get back to normal a little bit sooner.

People respect others who can own up to their mistakes and admit fault. Teach your children that if someone deserves an apology, it is their duty to acknowledge the wrongdoing by stating, "I'm really sorry. Please forgive me. That will not happen again." This skill will help your children in relationships throughout their entire lives.

BoostKids in Real Life:

In my home, Wendy and I have been able to instill this lesson rather effectively. When the kids do something wrong, it doesn't take much time for me to hear a sincere, "Dad, I'm really sorry. Will be you please forgive me?" instead of a disingenuous "sorry," that they know, and I know, is meaningless.

My kids have learned that it is not worth escalating a situation or problem from bad to worse by not saying they were sorry after upsetting us.

Tips:

1) Think of a time when your son did not issue a quick apology and a time when he did. Remind him how much quicker the situation was defused when he issued a prompt apology. In many cases, you can point out that the severity of his punishment decreased when he immediately confessed and asked for forgiveness.

2) Explain to your daughter that refusing or waiting to apologize will only increase the length and severity of her punishment. Also, talk about the long-term effects of such behavior. Explain that this character flaw will cost her friendships, relationships, and possibly a job in the future.

Lesson 28:
How to Handle Being Teased

> **"Man must evolve for all human conflict a method which rejects revenge, aggression, and retaliation. The foundation of such a method is love."**
>
> *Martin Luther King, Jr.*

 Being teased can be one of the most traumatic and stressful events in a kid's life. The type of teasing we are talking about is not good-natured ribbing between friends, but mean-spirited cruelty.

How children deal with being teased says a lot about their confidence, and is an indicator of how they will handle stress in the future.

If your child is being teased, here are a few suggestions to mentally and physically defeat the harassment:

Ignore

Let your son or daughter know that the bully is trying to incite a reaction. Explain that by ignoring the teaser, your child will start to turn the tables. If your son or daughter cannot be provoked, the bully will become frustrated and will likely stop.

Help your child realize that the bully is typically just insecure. Instill within them a mindset that says, "Why should I give that person the satisfaction of seeing me upset?"

"Thanks for Noticing" Response

If someone says, "Those are ugly shorts," your child may come back with something like, "Thank you for noticing my shorts." This expression of gratitude will throw teasers off balance, making them unsure of what to say next.

Return with a Compliment

If someone says, "You really swing the bat weird," your child can say, "You swing really well, what's your secret?" This time, your child can throw the teaser off balance with a compliment. The teaser will have no idea what hit him or her when your child demonstrates a behavior that rises above the intimidation tactics.

The Teaser is not Losing Sleep

Bullies don't care about your child's hurt feelings. So if the teaser is not losing sleep, neither should your son or daughter. Teach your child to think, "Hey! They are not being bothered by what they said, so why should I waste my energy feeling hurt?"

Growing up is difficult for kids. Work with them to develop techniques that they can utilize to ease the stress of being teased.

Tips:

1) Share stories about your childhood. Provide stories about times you were teased. Let your child know that although you were really upset when you were getting teased, it didn't really end up affecting your life.

2) If the situation escalates, talk to the teachers and principal at your child's school. Most schools today have bullying programs that can help defuse situations.

Tips to Keep in Mind When Teaching BoostKids

Now that you have completed the lesson portion, below are some tips for teaching BoostKids.

Offer Reminders behind the Scene

It is much more effective to remind your children of the skill that you want them to use before they are required to apply it in real-life situations. For example, if you are going out to eat, remind your child in the car ride to the restaurant to look the waiter or waitress in the eye when ordering. You do not want to make these suggestions at the restaurant in front of the server because this will only embarrass your child and make all the parties involved feel awkward and uncomfortable. After the waiter leaves, you can say, "Great job!" or, "You did not look him in the eye." It is much more productive to provide guidance and feedback before and after the real situation.

Make It Fun

When possible, try to make learning BoostKids fun. Many of the tips we suggest involve rewarding success with small prizes. Many of the BoostKids skills do not come naturally to children. So don't expect too much right away. The important point is that these skills and techniques need to be reinforced constantly, allowing them to sink in over time. Keep in mind that steady and sustained progress is the key. I know working with your child can be frustrating at times, but putting a smile on your face as much as possible will make the learning process enjoyable and impactful.

Stay Committed

As with anything else, it is easy to be energized and enthused about BoostKids, get started, and then quickly lose focus and get off track due to life's hectic schedule. Remember, this is not some gimmick we are talking about, but your child's future. BoostKids is too important to slip through the cracks! Please stay committed. The more you review these lessons, the more successful your child will become.

BoostKids Program Overview

BoostKids offers a comprehensive program that you and your child can use in the privacy of your home to learn the BoostKids lessons in a fun-filled approach. BoostKids also has programs designed for classroom or group settings. The BoostKids program is made up of the following components.

Interactive CD-ROM

The BoostKids CD-ROM is designed to make learning easy and fun for children. The CD-ROM contains video examples of kids in real-life scenarios demonstrating unacceptable behavior and demonstrating appropriate behavior. Interactive tests measure and monitor your child's progress from start to finish. In addition, the CD-ROM includes a special introduction for children and parents.

Audio CDs

So that adults and children can get a better feel for BoostKids, three parent CDs accompany three kid CDs, for a total of six audio CDs. The audio CDs are specifically tailored to the needs of the teacher (you, the parent) and pupil (your child). Specifically, BoostKids has prepared "Introductory" CDs that provide listeners with a broad overview of the program, as well as "Lessons" CDs that provide listeners with specific, detailed information about each of the twenty-eight BoostKids lessons. The CDs are perfect for listening in the car or on your iPod.

Student Activity Book

The BoostKids student workbook outlines all twenty-eight lessons in an easy-to-understand format that reinforces the messages seen on the CD-ROM and heard on the audio CDs.

Practice Cards

The BoostKids practice cards are designed to help parents review any of the twenty-eight lessons quickly with their children.

Bonus CD

The BoostKids Bonus CD is an audio CD that includes five additional lessons that compliment the twenty-eight primary BoostKids lessons. The lessons covered in the Bonus CD include:

- Dependability

- Outwork Them!

- Think Big

- Don't Be Afraid to Fail

- Leadership

The key to mastering the BoostKids lessons is practice and repetition. You want your children to hear the BoostKids message as many times as possible. Between the CD-ROM, the Audio CDs, the Student Activity Book, the Flash Cards, and the Bonus Lessons CD, we guarantee that the BoostKids program will teach your children life's most important lessons.

To order the BoostKids program, or if you would like more information, please go to www.boostkids.com. Also, feel free to email us at info@boostkids.com with any success stories, suggestions, or questions.

www.boostkids.com

NOTES

1) Goleman, *Emotional Intelligence: Why It Can Matter More Than IQ* (New York: Bantam Books, 1996).

2) Robert Orben (1927–), American author.

3) Twenge, Ph.D. and W. Keith Campbell, Ph.D., *The Narcissism Epidemic: Living in the Age of Entitlement* (New York: Free Press, 2009).

4) Seligman, Ph.D., *The Optimistic Child* (New York: Houghton Mifflin, 1995).

REFERENCES

Goleman, Daniel. *Emotional Intelligence: Why It Can Matter More Than IQ* (New York: Bantam Books, 1996).

Seligman, Martin E.P., Ph.D. *The Optimistic Child* (New York: Houghton Mifflin, 1995).

Twenge, Jean M., Ph.D. and W. Keith Campbell, Ph.D. *The Narcissism Epidemic: Living in the Age of Entitlement (*New York: Free Press, 2009).